EPIC ACHIEVEMENTS AGAINST INCREDIBLE ODDS

How America's Greatest Engineering Marvels Were Built During Her Darkest Days

Steve McCurdy

Copyright

CONTENTS

Prologue

Book I – The Epic Achievements

Book II – The Rise & Fall of American Greatness

PROLOGUE

It was a good day. The Powell Shopper, our weekly local newspaper, announced that the state was building a bypass that would divert 10,000 cars a day away from Emory Road, the busy thoroughfare which runs right through the heart of our little town. The bike trail I use crosses Emory Road three times outbound and three times coming back home. I have had my share of hair-raising crossings over the years, so the new bypass gave me something to cheer about.

Tentatively named the "Powell Connector," the new road would be 2.4 miles long, and its primary feature would be a 200 yard long bridge over the Southern Railway tracks. The roadbed ran through relatively flat, undeveloped land until it neared the railroad tracks ,where it rose gently until it bridged the tracks and reconnected with Emory Road about two miles east of my house. The finished road would leave my bike trail pretty much traffic-free, at least in the early mornings when I did my riding.

Before long equipment started to show up at the worksite, and because I had a good vantage point and a keen interest, I kept close tabs on the progress of the work. The bridge was finished in about six months, and although I am not a bridge builder, that seemed to me like a reasonable amount of time.

But then everything changed. We went from full speed ahead to super slow mo. The proposed roadbed was by then lined with flatbed trucks, bulldozers, giant scrapers and water trucks, but they didn't move and we seldom saw any sign of life. Sometimes weeks and even months would pass without any sightings of a warm body on the site. I soon became cynical and began to obsess a little bit about the project, and my wife's eyes began to roll back in her head whenever the subject came up. Soon a year had passed, and then two.

4

Most of my immediate family lives near our house and we all get together every Sunday for a BBQ. Before long the Powell connector became the primary topic of conversation at our Sunday get-togethers. To vent my frustration and liven up the gatherings, I would pick one of America's famous construction projects from history each Sunday and then compare it with the Powell connector. The projects I chose all had two things in common – first they were completed in less time than it was taking to build the connector, and second, the projects were so incredible that even comparing them to the connector was laughable. For example, one Sunday I talked about how in 1867, 12,000 Chinese laborers (then called "coolies") built tunnels through the Sierra Nevada Mountains for the transcontinental railroad. To build the infamous "Summit Tunnel 6" on Donner Pass, they drilled and blasted through almost a half mile of solid granite in brutal weather conditions in less than a year, without benefit of electricity or power tools. How, I would ask my kids, could those Chinese laborers possibly have accomplished that unbelievable feat 150 years ago in less than half the time it is taking us today to build a two-mile road with a million dollars worth of equipment?

Soon, everyone in the family began to kind of look forward to hearing about another project each week (at least they told me they did), and I found myself spending more and more time finding great stories and doing research. I discovered that behind every iconic American engineering masterpiece there was one person, one driving force, whose vision and passion inspired his team to overcome incredible challenges and adversity as they constructed architectural wonders.

I decided to write about some of these mostly forgotten Americans, who most readers will probably have never heard of, and this book is the result.

Frank Crowe received his engineering degree from the University of Maine in 1905 and immediately headed west. Thirty years later he had built 15 of the world's greatest dams, including the colossal Hoover Dam. His work opened up millions of acres of the American West to human settlement. After World War II ended, Crowe was asked by the United States Secretary of War to head up the effort to rebuild Germany, but had to decline due to ill health.

German immigrant John Roebling figured out how to "spin" wires into huge steel cables, and in doing so invented the suspension bridge. Roebling designed and built the Brooklyn Bridge in 1863, and his Company "John Roebling & Sons Wire Rope Company" would be instrumental in building virtually every suspension bridge in the country, including the famed George Washington Bridge in 1931 and the majestic Golden Gate Bridge in 1937.

An architect-turned-contractor named Paul Starrett perfected the art of the skyscraper, and used his organizational genius to build the Empire State Building in the incredibly short time of just 444 days - groundbreaking to grand opening. The Empire State was the world's tallest for thirty-seven years, and today remains Manhattan's most famous landmark. Modern day structural engineers still marvel at Starrett's accomplishment.

General Brehon Burke Somervell was the unsung hero of World War II. He managed the greatest mobilization of men and materials in the history of mankind when the United States entered the war, and in his spare time he built the world's largest building - the Pentagon, and had it ready for occupancy seven months after ground was broken. Somervell's motto was "We do the impossible immediately. The miraculous takes a little longer."

From the time he was eight years old, William Francis Gibbs had one goal in life, and that was to build the world's greatest

ship. As the sun rose on the morning of May 14, 1952, just after Gibbs had turned 66 years of age, the great engines of the
1,000 foot long SS United States came to life and she pulled
out to sea. On her maiden transatlantic voyage she broke
Queen Mary's crossing speed record by more than 10 hours,
and her legendary records for speed and safety would never
be challenged by any other ship.

As I learned more about these American giants and their legacy projects, I realized that they all dated from the same
twenty-plus year period 1931 to 1952, a period that now
probably qualifies as being "back in the day." I theorized that
maybe the decline in these remarkable projects mirrors
America's decline generally, and I began to wonder what
caused the slide and whether the country will ever be able
bounce back and enable us to start building again. As you will
learn in later chapters, I am cautiously hopeful.

But be that as it may, all is not lost. After more than three
years as a work in progress, the Powell connecter is finally
finished. After the contractor paid daily late penalties for a
month and a half, he finally sent a crew over and finished up
the job. I doubt that anyone will ever write a book about the
connector, but my bike rides are now much safer.

CHAPTER 1

HOOVER DAM

THE CHALLENGE – TAMING THE RAGING RIVER

In the late 1800s the Colorado River was the principal river in the Southwestern United States. The 1,450-mile river, known for its dramatic canyons and whitewater rapids, drained a 246,000 square mile watershed encompassing an area now covering parts of seven U.S. states. Rising in the Rocky Mountains, the river flowed southwest across the Colorado Plateau and through the Grand Canyon before reaching what is now the Arizona–Nevada line, where it turned south toward the international border. After entering Mexico, the Colorado emptied into the Gulf of California between Baja California and Sonora.

In 1900, developers decided that the Imperial Valley of southern California would be an excellent location to develop agriculture if it could be irrigated by the waters of the Colorado. They hired an engineer named George Chaffey to design the Alamo Canal, which split off from the Colorado River near Pilot Knob, curved south into Mexico, and dumped into the Alamo River, a dry arroyo which had historically carried the flood waters of the Colorado into the Valley.[1] They then began large-scale farming, and small towns in the region started to grow with the influx of job-seeking migrants. By 1903, more than 100,000 acres in the valley were under cultivation, supporting a growing population of 4,000.

But soon the temperamental Colorado River began to wreak havoc with its unpredictable flows. In early 1905, heavy floods destroyed the headworks of the Alamo Canal, and water began to flow uncontrolled down the Canal towards the

8

Salton Sink. On August 9, the entire flow of the Colorado swerved into the Canal and began to flood the bottom of the Imperial Valley.[2] Desperate to close the breach, crews of the Southern Pacific Railroad, whose tracks ran through the valley, attempted to dam the Colorado above the Canal, only to see their work demolished by another flood. It took seven attempts, more than $3 million, and two years for the railroad, the Imperial Valley developers, and the federal government to permanently block the breach and send the Colorado on its natural course to the gulf – but not before part of the Imperial Valley was flooded under a 45-mile-long lake, today known as the Salton Sea.[3] Officials realized then that a more permanent solution would be required to rein in the raging Colorado River. In 1922, six U.S. states in the Colorado River basin signed the Colorado River Compact, dividing the river's flow among the states.[4] This Compact, and several others which followed, formed the basis for what is now known as the "Law of the River."

ENTER MASTER DAM BUILDER FRANK CROWE

Frank Crowe was born October 12, 1882, in Trenholmville, Quebec. His family moved to Massachusetts in 1888, and Crowe enrolled in the University of Maine in 1901 to study civil engineering. In his last year at Maine, Crowe listened to several lectures by Frank Weymouth, a Bureau of Reclamation ("BOR") engineer. Weymouth described the Bureau's ambitious plans to "reclaim" the West with major dams and irrigation projects, and Crowe was hooked. He took a job with the Bureau of Reclamation when he finished school, and headed West without waiting for his graduation ceremony.[5]

During his tenure with the Bureau of Reclamation Crowe developed a reputation as a mechanical genius, and he became known as the Government's best construction man. He also picked up a nickname "Hurry-Up Crowe" which stuck with him for life.[6] While supervising construction of Arrowdock

Dam, Crowe pioneered two techniques which moved dam construction out of the era of mules and scrapers, and revolutionized the methodology of building big dams. The first was a system of pipe grids which could transport concrete pneumatically, and the second was an overhead cableway system which could rapidly make pinpoint concrete deliveries to any point on a dam. Using these and other innovations he developed, Crowe would build nineteen dams over his illustrious career, but none of the others approached the mythic scale of the Hoover Dam.[7]

The Boulder Dam Project became an obsession with Crowe beginning in 1919, when he roughed out a cost estimate for damming the Colorado with Arthur Powell Davis, nephew of famous explorer John Wesley Powell. In 1921, Crowe reportedly told his father "I'm going to build the Boulder Dam."[8] During this same period Crowe also worked with Walker Young, who would become the construction engineer on Boulder Dam, and, in 1924 Crowe actually helped Young with preliminary designs for the Dam.[9]

In 1925, the BOR changed its modus operandi from doing its own dam construction to contracting all the work out.[10] Frank Crowe, already known as the world's best dam builder, wanted to continue to build dams and had no intention of becoming a bureaucrat. His motto was "never my belly to a desk," and he resigned from the BOR after 20 years.[11] Crowe then went to work for Morrison-Knudsen Construction Company in Boise, Idaho, primarily because Morrison-Knudsen had recently joined forces with Utah Construction Company to build dams.

On December 21, 1928 President Coolidge signed the bill authorizing the Boulder Dam. "The Boulder Canyon Project Act" appropriated $165 million for the Hoover Dam along with the Imperial Dam downstream and the All-American Canal, a replacement for the Alamo Canal entirely on the U.S. side of the border. It also permitted the compact to go into effect as soon as at least six of the seven states approved it. The sixth approval was obtained on March 6, 1929, with Utah's ratification.[12]

On January 10, 1931, the BOR made the bid documents available to interested parties for five dollars a copy. At the suggestion of BOR chief design engineer John L. Savage, the dam would be a concrete, arch gravity structure. The government was to provide the materials; but the contractor was to prepare the site and build the dam. The dam was described in minute detail in a document that covered 100 pages of text and included 76 drawings. A $2 million bid bond was to accompany each bid, and the winner would have to post a $5 million performance bond. Whoever was awarded the contract would be given seven years to complete the dam without late penalties.[13]

Everything Crowe had ever done in his career had prepared him to build Hoover Dam, and his dream was about to become the biggest challenge of his life.[14] The first thing he did was to convince Harry Morrison, Morrison-Knudsen's President, that no one company possessed the financial resources, the experience, and the know-how to do the whole project. He recommended that they put together a consortium of companies

----

Note: The terms "Hoover Dam" and "Boulder Dam" are used interchangeably herein. The dam was officially called Hoover Dam from July, 1930, until May, 1933, when the name was officially changed to Boulder Dam. The name was changed back to Hoover Dam by Congress on April 30, 1947.

----

which together possessed all the capabilities and resources necessary to undertake the massive project, and which could split the performance bond.

To bid on the dam, Morrison and Crowe assembled a joint venture called the "Six Companies," which were Morrison-Knudsen, Utah Construction Company (Wattis Brothers) (railroad construction), JF Shea Company (plumbing & underground tunnels), Pacific Bridge Company (bridges), McDonald & Kahn (buildings), and Kaiser & Bechtel (road building).[15]

Six Companies executives. Frank Crowe is 3rd from right.

The Six Companies appointed Crowe their dam Construction Superintendant and won the contract with a bid of $48.9 million for the project. The bid, which Crowe had personally prepared, was just $24,000 higher than the staff of the Department of the Interior had themselves budgeted for the project, and it was $5 million lower than the next lowest bid.[16]

At the time, the contract was the largest ever awarded by the United States government.[17]

BUILDING THE DAM

Work Force

The country was already mired in the initial stages of what would become the Great Depression, and word of a massive new construction project lured desperate job seekers and their families to Southern Nevada from far and wide. Las Vegas, then a small city of some 5,000, saw between 10,000 and 20,000 unemployed newcomers descend upon it, most of whom lived in tents.

A government camp was established for surveyors and other personnel near the dam site, and soon a squatters' camp, known as McKeeversville, was set up nearby. Another squatters' camp, on the flats along the Colorado River, was officially called Williamsville, but was known to its inhabitants as Ragtown. It was summer in the desert, and the tent communities were a living hell, with poor sanitation, little access to clean water, 119 degree heat, and no utilities.[18]

Dam workers sharing a tent in Ragtown - 1931

Crowe understood full well that a qualified work force could not be assembled without acceptable living conditions, and the original timetable required Six Companies to build a town called Boulder City to house the workers before the project began. However, when President Hoover ordered work on the dam to begin in March rather than in October, Boulder City had to wait.

Until Boulder City was completed, workers with families were left to provide their own accommodations and many lived in Ragtown. Sixteen Ragtown residents died of heat prostration between June 25 and July 26, 1931. When Boulder City finally opened in late 1931, living conditions began to improve and the new town eventually included utilities, a school, a church, a post office, a library, stores, and even a newspaper.[19]

Once construction began, Six Companies hired large numbers of workers, with more than 3,000 on the payroll by the beginning of 1932, and with employment peaking at 5,251 in July 1934.[20] At peak employment the daily payroll was $21,674 for 5,251 men, which was an average of $4.13 per day per man, equivalent to about $70 today. Throughout virtually the entire project men worked around the clock in three shifts, and there were only two days each year when work shut down – July 4, and Christmas.[21]

The Diversion Tunnels

Before dam concrete could be poured, the river had to be diverted away from the construction site. To do that, four diversion tunnels, two on each side of the river, would have to be drilled through solid rock. The tunnels would be round, each with a diameter of 56 feet. In total, the tunnels would be a little more than three miles long. After the tunnels were drilled, the walls would be covered with a three foot wide blanket of concrete, reducing their overall diameters to 50 feet. Crowe regarded the diversion tunnels as the most challenging and difficult phase of the project.[22]

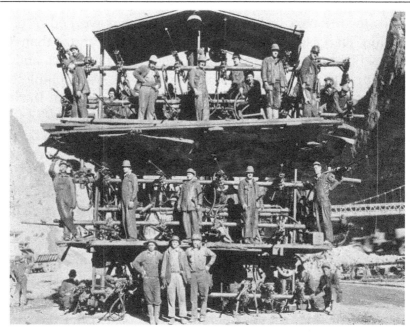

A Williams Jumbo Driller

The contract allowed 28 months for completion of the diversion tunnels, with a deadline of October 1, 1933. From the standpoint of scheduling, the actual tunnel drilling presented Crowe with his toughest challenge. Because the drills had to be horizontal and the tunnels were 56 feet high, scaffolding would be required for the drillers to stand on. Since each drill would only penetrate 16 feet of rock, the scaffolding would have to continually be assembled, taken down, and reassembled, burning enormous amounts of unproductive time and making the deadline almost impossible to meet. To meet this challenge Crowe's Deputy Superintendent Woody Williams came up with "scaffolding on wheels." Permanent steel scaffolding was mounted on the bed of large trucks to create "jumbo drillers" that would accommodate up to thirty drills on three levels.[23] When each drill segment was completed and the dynamite charges prepared, the trucks would simply back away, wait for the dynamite blast, then move back into

15

place for the next drill segment. The jumbos worked to perfection, increasing the pace of the drilling by more than 10 times. Eight jumbos were utilized, one working at each end of all four tunnels. By the time the drilling was completed, Crowe's men were working with military precision. During the last full month of drilling, they blasted through 6,773 feet of rock, representing over 40% of the total tunneling.[24] Largely due to the "Jumbos," the tunnels were completed almost a year ahead of schedule. Crowe now faced what he believed was the toughest part of the tunneling job – the actual diversion. He had built many dams and diverted many rivers, but never one like the Colorado.

Temporary cofferdams had been built in the river channel to block water from the diversion tunnels while they were being built, and a trestle bridge spanned the river 100 feet upstream from the tunnel openings. Now, the cofferdam protecting the Arizona side tunnels would be blown apart by dynamite, and simultaneously a new cofferdam would be built under the trestle bridge to block the main channel and divert its flow into the Arizona diversion tunnels. The Nevada diversion tunnels would not be needed until spring floods came down the river.

It was November and the river was at low ebb. The six companies had called in every truck they owned that could haul rock and gravel, and all the fully-loaded trucks were parked on the river bank near the bridge. At 11:30 am on Armistice Day in 1932 an enormous blast shook the canyon as the cofferdam was dynamited. Shortly after the blast, the long procession of trucks began dropping their loads of rock from the trestle bridge. For fifteen straight hours the trucks dropped rock and gravel into the river at the rate of 15 tons per minute. By dawn on November 14, 1932, the Colorado had given up and the water was flowing directly into the Arizona diversion tunnels. The hard part was over, and Crowe was almost a year ahead of schedule.[25]

A Diversion Tunnel, prior to being lined with 3' concrete walls

Bedrock Preparation

It was essential for the dam to rest on virgin, solid bedrock, not only at its base but also against the canyon side walls. The dam was an "arch gravity" dam, and its convex side faced the tremendous force of the impounded lake. That meant that the sidewalls of the canyon would bear the brunt of the lake's force. Over the centuries the surface rock had been subjected to constant wind, rain, snow and high winds, and the resulting "weathering" created loose rocks, erosion materials, cracks, crevices and fissures, all of which would preclude the production of water-tight seams. Therefore the sidewalls had to be cleared or "groomed" to remove the weathered material and get down to virgin rock, and the sidewall "grooming" presented another unique challenge.

The grooming had to be done by men sitting in bosun's chairs suspended hundreds of feet above the canyon floor on long, one inch diameter hemp ropes. The ropes enabled workers to move up and down the canyon walls and to swing back and forth across their face. The men were equipped with jack-hammers, drills and dynamite.

The groomers became known as "high scalers." Many of them were members of nearby Indian tribes, who had little inherent fear of heights and were accomplished rock climbers. The high scalers became popular attractions for dam visitors and the media, and were known for showing off for the crowds below by swinging back and

Famed High Scalers from among nearby indian tribes

forth across the canyon face. But there was no mistaking that their work was dangerous, and they were among the Dam's highest paid workers.[26]

Objects falling from above represented the biggest hazard for the high scalers, and to protect themselves, they dipped cloth hats in hot tar, and then allowed them to harden. When it was proven that these "tar hats" provided effective protection, the Six Companies ordered thousands of what have since become known as "hardhats."[27]

Grooming the sidewalls was not dependent upon the diversion tunnels, so the high scaler's work continued for more than two years from the project's beginning until the first concrete pour in June, 1933.

Water-tight seams were also required at the dam's base. It was necessary to excavate for the Dam's foundation by completely clearing the exposed riverbed to enable the Dam to rest on bedrock. This part of the process was done by conventional means, using derricks and dump trucks. When the foundation work was completed in June of 1933, approximately 1,500,000 cubic feet yards of material had been removed from the Colorado riverbed.[28]

The cleared, bedrock foundation and walls of the canyon then had to be reinforced with what was called "grout curtains." All seams, particularly at the Dam's base, had to be watertight. Any unobstructed pathways for water seepage would create a condition known as "uplift." Uplift was upward pressure from water seeping under the dam, and extreme uplift could theoretically cause upward pressure strong enough to actually tip a dam over.

A total of 393 holes, some as deep as 150' into the rock, were to be drilled and any cavities encountered were to be filled with grout to stabilize the rock and prevent seepage. All the drillers were under extreme time pressures to complete the work for the beginning of the concrete pour. Unfortunately, some of them, when they encountered hot springs or cavities which were too large to readily fill, simply moved on without resolving the problem. Fifty-eight of the 393 holes (15% of them) were not completely filled.[29]

This problem was unbeknownst to Crowe and was not discovered until large numbers of significant leaks appeared after the dam was complete and the lake was filling. It ultimately took nine years for a small team of men, working pretty much in secrecy, to complete the grout curtain and stabilize the dam.

Pouring the Dam

The Dam could not be built using a continuous concrete pour for several compelling reasons. First was heat and curing. Hardening of concrete is a chemical process that generates great heat, causing it to expand. Had the dam been built with a continuous pour it would have taken 125 years for the concrete mass to cure, and the concrete would have expanded, broken and crumbled in the process.[30] The second factor preventing a continuous pour was that many different grades of concrete were used, each grade requiring different aggregate rock. The aggregate ranged in size from pea gravel (used on outside facings) to smoothed, nine inch cobblestones (used toward the center of the mass).

The third factor restricting the pour was the requirement that the entire mass of concrete had to be crisscrossed with cooling pipes through which cold water could be pumped, and there were also more than 800 thermometers and other glass-encased instruments that had to be placed in the concrete at predetermined intervals and then connected to a monitoring system. There were also grout valves, water drains, and molds for the internal inspection galleries (15 each of five levels), as well as two 600 foot elevator shafts and two 600 foot spiral staircases. Hoover Dam was the most heavily instrumented Dam in history.

So instead of one continuous pour, the concrete in the Dam was poured into 230, different-sized, pre-formed columns, some of which were as large as 50' by 50.' The concrete was all poured in 5' high units, which were called "lifts." Once poured into its column, each five foot lift was identified by a unique alpha numeric block number. Each block had to cure for 72 hours before the next lift could be poured. The 1" thin-walled, steel cooling pipes were laid on the top surface of each block, so each 5' block had cooling pipes beneath it and on top of it. A 50' X 50' X 5' block contained 12,500 cubic feet of concrete.[32]

Ready to pour a lift with a Crowe Bucket – 1934

The concrete was poured into the columns from "Crowe Buckets" which were cylindrical buckets 7' high and 7' in diameter, each of which held 16 tons of wet concrete (about 208 cubic feet).[33] The concrete was mixed at one of two onsite concrete plants, and poured into the Crowe buckets, which were then positioned on railroad cars in one of the nine trains which transported the concrete to the site. The railroad track hung on the Nevada canyon wall, 220 feet above the riverbed. The nine trains were making a constant loop delivering the buckets to the cable way terminus and taking the empties back for refilling. At the cableway terminus each bucket was hoisted onto one of five cableways, and then signalmen and operators moved each bucket into proper position above the appropriate column. When the bucket was properly positioned, the concrete workers on the column whacked the latches at the bottom of the bucket with their shovels, releasing the sixteen tons of wet concrete. The first bucket poured on each new lift was pure grout, to ensure a strong bond with next lift.

The first Crowe bucket was poured from cableway 6 on June 6, 1933, into block number J-3, located on the dam's centerline three sections in from its face. The pouring continued for

625 consecutive days, until the last pour was made at the dam's crest on February 21, 1935. The BOR had allotted 32 months for the pour, but Crowe had completed it in less than 21 months.[34]

One of the true marvels of the project was the concrete cooling system. When completed, the dam contained more than 600 miles of cooling pipes. The objective of the pipes was to reduce the temperature of the curing concrete to 45^0 Fahrenheit, and this was done in two stages. The first stage circulated cool river water through the pipes to extract half the unwanted heat from the mass. In the second phase, the water was sent through a refrigeration plant on the Nevada side to lower its temperature to 40^0. This system reduced a fifty foot section (10 lifts) to the desired temperature in six to eight weeks. After the desired temperature was reached in each 50' section, the thin-walled pipes were filled with grout, thereby creating a network of internal expansion joints.

Concrete was poured in columns, which can be seen here

Appurtenant Structures

As work on the dam progressed a number of appurtenant structures were being built nearby in the canyon. Principal among these were the following:

Intake Towers and Penstocks

On the upstream side, close to the Dam itself, are four cylindrical intake towers. Each 390-foot intake tower delivers water from Lake Meade into a penstock, which is a giant steel tube with a 30' diameter. As the water pours 500 feet down the penstock (the "head") on its way to the powerhouse it reaches a speed of 85 mph.35 The roaring water is diverted from the penstock into one of 17 smaller tunnels ("adits") by wicket gates which take it directly to one of the Dam's turbines. The water turns the turbine, and the turbine's shaft fuels the power generator. After going through the turbines the water emerges back into the River on the downstream side. Every drop of water released through the dam passes through the turbines, generates electricity, and returns to the river.

Powerhouse

The powerhouse is a U-shaped building at the base of the dam on the downstream side. Each wing of the U is 650 feet long and 300 feet tall. The powerhouse has 10 acres of floor space which houses the Dam's seventeen turbines and power generators. The roof of the powerhouse is bomb-proof, with layers of concrete, rock, and steel 3.5 feet thick. The average, annual power generation of the Dam is 4.2 billion kilowatt hours, and the power is purchased by 15 different political jurisdictions and utilities.[36]

Spillways

Two spillways were constructed, one behind each side of the Dam, to protect against overtopping of the Dam during floods. Each spillway has four 100' X 16' steel gates which can be raised or lowered depending upon water levels. Each of the gates weighs 2,500 tons, and can be operated manually or automatically. Water flowing over the spillways drops 600' into wide spillway tunnels which connect with the original outer diversion tunnels before reentering the main river channel. Except for testing, the spillways have only had be used once, during the flooding of 1983.[37] [40] Each one of the Dam's two spillways can handle a volume of water equal to that spilling over Niagara Falls, making the Dam virtually floodproof.

Babcock & Wilcox Steel Foundry

Fabrication of the Dam's four enormous penstocks posed special logistics problems for the project. The required, 30 foot diameter of the penstocks meant that they were simply too large to be transported to the site on any existing US railroad or highway. Accordingly, it was decided that they had to be fabricated on site.

Having foreseen this challenge prior to soliciting bids, the BOR had carved $11 million out of the contract for the fabrication job. The Bureau paid Babcock & Wilcox, an Ohio-based manufacturer of steel pressure boilers, to build a steel foundry on the site. Babcock & Wilcox built a huge foundry, 670 feet long and five stories tall, less than a mile from the Dam site. The plant employed 800 workers.[38]

Even though they were built on-site, the team still faced the daunting challenge of moving the penstock sections (each section weighing 170 tons) over the 1 mile distance from the foundry to the canyon. To accomplish this, the Bureau commissioned the building of a special wide roadway and an extra-wide steel trailer with its own steering and braking system. At the canyon rim the sections were handed off to a government-built, 200 ton-capacity cable system to lower the sections into place.

THE COMPLETED DAM – A MONUMENT TO HUMAN ACHIEVEMENT

Hoover Dam was dedicated by President Franklin Delano Roosevelt on September 20, 1935. The Dam had been completed in only 1,660 days, a mind-boggling 895 days, or two and a half years, ahead of schedule. More than 200 engineers contributed to the design of the Dam and over 21,000 men worked on it over the course of its construction. The Dam is 726 feet high and 1,244 feet wide. It is 660 feet thick at its base and 45 feet thick at its crest.[39] The Dam's total weight is approximately 6.6 million tons, and it contains more than 91.8 billion cubic feet of concrete, enough to build a two lane highway from Seattle to Miami.

Hoover Dam impounds Lake Meade, the largest man-made lake in the United States, covering 250 square miles with 550 miles of shoreline. Ten million people annually visit Lake Meade and seven million visit the Dam itself.

POST-CONSTRUCTION ECONOMICS

Hoover Dam is not only an engineering marvel and a visual wonder, but it is also an economic powerhouse.

The all-in cost of building Hoover Dam was approximately $165 million, and it was completed in 1935. In 2015 dollars, the Dam's cost would be about $2.805 billion.

The Dam's two primary purposes were water distribution and flood control. It is not possible to place an exact dollar amount on the Dam's actual contribution to these goals without also considering all the dams downstream from Hoover, but it is estimated that water flowing through Hoover eventually irrigates more than 1 million acres of land, and that the water impounded in Lake Meade benefits 8 million people in Arizona, Nevada, and California.

Although water control, and not power generation, was always the primary purpose of the dam, it is power generation that has allowed the Dam to be self-sustaining. Every ounce of the water that passes through the Dam turns the turbines and generates power. Hydroelectricity is a clean and renewable source of energy. It does not create air pollution, chemical runoff, or toxic waste, and after the water does its job in the Powerhouse it re-enters the river and heads downstream to the next Dam to do its work all over again.

The Dam's seventeen turbines have produced an average of 4.2 billion kilowatt hours of hydroelectric power annually since 1961,[41] when all seventeen generators began operating in tandem. The power is pre-sold on a contractual basis to fifteen political jurisdictions and utilities in three states, and it serves 1.3 million users.[42] The five largest purchasers of Hoover Dam's power output are:

Metro Water District - Southern California 28.5393%

The State of Nevada   23.3706%

The State of Arizona   18.9527%

Los Angeles, Califonia 15.4229%

Southern California Edison 5.5377%

Actual rates are negotiated by the BOR with each purchaser, but the average retail price of electricity per kilowatt hour in the United States is 12¢, meaning that the economic value of an average year's power output at the Dam is $504 million. So, if the Hoover Dam's output were sold at average retail, the Dam would pay for itself every 5.56 years.

LASTING CULTURAL LEGACY

From the very beginning the Hoover Dam project faced seemingly insurmountable logistical challenges. The remote location of the worksite required that an entire infrastructure of power, water, roads, railways, and housing be installed before work could even begin.

As work progressed, the sheer size and scope of the project presented engineers with a constant stream of challenges, each one of which had to be overcome before work could proceed. These challenges resulted in the development of innovative new equipment, specialized cooling processes, and improved construction techniques that would influence dam building for decades to come. Perhaps just as important, the Dam also demonstrated that man could beneficially alter his environment and improve the quality of life for its inhabitants.

Since its completion in 1935 Hoover Dam has brought vitality to the American West. The Dam provides reliable and economical supplies of water and power to the states of Nevada,

Arizona and California, making possible the dramatic munici-
pal growth that all three states have enjoyed. Without the
Dam it is unlikely that we would find the names Los Angeles,
Phoenix and Las Vegas on today's lists of greatest American
cities.

Credit for this remarkable achievement should be spread
among all of the 200 engineers and 21,000 thousand workers
who worked on the Dam. Most of them are no longer living,
but it is well known among chroniclers of the Dam that many
of these men regarded their work on the Dam as the most
meaningful period in their lives.[43]

But as much as Hoover Dam is a monument to all the men
who built it, it is also a monument to the one indispensible
man, the visionary engineering genius and consummate man-
ager of men without whom the Dam could not have been
built. That man was Frank "Hurry-Up" Crowe.

Here are some remembrances of Frank Crowe:

*"Everybody who worked down here knew who Frank Crowe
was. Very tall and erect, kind of stately looking person, a very
likeable fellow, He was all over the job. His workmen, he knew
them by their first names, nearly every one of them...if he
wasn't in the office, he was down on the dam. It'd never surprise
me to see to see him down there at 2 o'clock in the morning,
looking around...if something went wrong he was there...to ex-
plain what went wrong, fix it. He was there to help you, not fire
you."*[44]

Saul "Red Wixon" an employee on Hoover Dam

*"Frank was an audacious problem solver. Once when cut timber
could not be procured at the Jackson Lake work site, he ordered
an entire sawmill from Salt Lake City and had it floated to the
construction site by barge."*[45]

Anonymous, from Collosus, Hiltzik

"Frank Crowe was not only an engineering genius, he was a genius for organized thinking and for imparting organized thinking to other people."[46]

Employee Elton Garrett

"He used innovation, motivation, and inspiration to turn a ragtag army of unemployed men into builders of the greatest monument to American industrial might of its day."[47]

PBS "The American Experience" Television's most-watched history series.

"His projects will stand forever as monuments to his great ability as a constructor, but he will be best remembered by his many friends and close associates for his ever-present human understanding, his extreme fair-mindedness, his wonderful sense of humor, and his absolute integrity – once his word was given it was carried out, no matter what the personal sacrifices might be."[48]

American Society of Civil Engineers in a memorial essay and eulogy – 1946

Frank Crowe

Frank Crowe walked away from his amazing accomplishment at Hoover Dam with a bonus of $350,000, equivalent to more than $5 million today.[49] He built four more dams, bringing his total to nineteen, but none would surpass Hoover as his crowning career achievement. In 1944 Frank Crowe retired to his 20,000 acre ranch near Redding, California.

At the end of World War II Crowe received an offer from the United States Secretary of War Robert W. Patterson to become Engineer-In-Charge of the reconstruction of Germany. Unbeknownst to the general public, he had survived a heart attack earlier that year, and as a result he turned down the offer. Crowe suffered a second heart attack at this ranch, this one fatal, in 1946.

Frank Crowe remained modest and self-effacing throughout his life, and always spurned adulation. He once told an interviewer that *"If you want to see the fellow who really built this dam, go over to the mess hall. He wears a tin hat, his average age is 31, and he can do things."* Frank Crowe left no memoirs or written histories, but preferred instead to let his work speak for itself.[51]

On October 22, 1955 Hoover Dam was named one of "America's Seven Modern Civil Engineering Wonders" by the American Society of Civil Engineers ("ASCE"), and in 2001[52] the ASCE included Hoover Dam on its list of the "Top 10 Civil Engineering Monuments of the Millenium."[53]

Many of the millions who have visited the Hoover Dam know it as America's version of the Great Pyramids of Egypt.

CHAPTER 2

THE GOLDEN GATE BRIDGE

THE CHALLENGE – BRIDGING THE STRAIT

The idea of bridging the strait between San Francisco and Marin County had excited imaginations since the mid-1800s. Connecting San Francisco and Marin County could be a huge boon for the Bay Area. San Francisco was the largest American city still accessed primarily by ferry boat, and its growth rate was below the national average. But bridging the Strait was a daunting challenge. Many contractors and engineers in that day did not believe that the Golden Gate Strait could ever be bridged. The challenges it presented boggled the mind.

No bridge had ever been built at a harbor entrance, primarily because any structure would have to be high enough to allow the passage of the largest ships in the world at high tide. A bridge in this particular harbor would face almost constant, 50 mph winds hitting it broadside, and it would be shrouded in dense fog much of the time. The strait separating San Francisco from Marin County was over a mile wide. Geologically, it was really a gorge in a mountain range. The gorge was 335' deep, and incoming water from the Pacific Ocean met outgoing water from San Francisco Bay, producing swirling tides and violent, temperamental currents.[1]

To further complicate the project, it would be located less than eight miles from the epicenter of the most catastrophic earthquake in history.

Prior to construction of the bridge, the only practical route between San Francisco and Marin County was by ferry boat across a section of the San Francisco Bay. The Sausalito Land

and Ferry Company, a subsidiary of the Southern Pacific Railroad, had been renamed the Golden Gate Ferry Company, and by the 1920s it was the largest ferry operation in the world. It traversed the distance between the Hyde Street Pier in SF and Sausalito in approximately 20 minutes for a price of $1.[2]

Legend has it that in 1872, while the Brooklyn Bridge was under construction, an entrepreneur named Charles Crocker had actually submitted plans and cost estimates for a Golden Gate bridge, but in 1916 James Wilkins made what is regarded as the first serious proposal. Wilkins was a structural engineer, and he took his proposal to SF City Engineer Michael O'Shaughnessy.[3] O'Shaughnessy became an advocate for the bridge, and in 1918 the SF Board of Supervisors asked Congress to authorize a federal survey of the Golden Gate Channel. The USS Natoma survey ship sounded the channel and submitted the data to O'Shaughnessy.[4] He in turn submitted the data to three nationally-known bridge builders.

Gustav Lindenthal (May 21, 1850 – July 31, 1935) was a civil engineer who designed the Hell Gate Bridge in New York City, among other bridges. Lindenthal's work was greatly affected by his pursuit for perfection and his love of art. His structures not only served the purpose they were designed for, but were aesthetically pleasing to the eye. Lindenthal submitted a minimum estimate of $56 million.

Francis Charles McMath (1867-February 13, 1938) was an American engineer and amateur astronomer. He became successful in the bridge-building industry, and was president of the Canadian Bridge and Iron Company in Detroit. McMath never formally responded to O'Shaughnessy's inquiry.

The third recipient of O'Shaughnssey's inquiry was Joseph Bearman Strauss.

JOSEPH BEARMAN STRAUSS – A BRIDGE-BUILDING POET

Joseph Strauss was born into an artistic family in Cincinnati in 1870. Though he gained renown as an engineer, he continued to write poetry all his life. Strauss attended the University of Cincinnati, and while in the infirmary recovering from a football injury, Strauss stared out his window at the Cincinnati-Covington Suspension Bridge, which at the time was the world's longest span and which was built by John A. Roebling, arguably the foremost figure in the history of bridge building.[5] Roebling's Company built the Brooklyn Bridge and would later be named a major contractor for the Golden Gate Bridge. That visual experience from his hospital window developed a deep fascination with bridges that would guide Strauss's life.

Strauss was Senior Class President in college, and for his senior thesis he had presented a proposal to build an international railroad that would span the 55-mile wide Bering Strait over a bridge that would join Alaska and Russia.[6] His paper demonstrated that he was not afraid of "thinking big."

Seven years after graduating Strauss designed his trademark "bascule" drawbridge template. His drawbridges were practical and utilitarian, but not visually appealing. Strauss formed the Strauss Bascule Bridge Company in 1904 to build his bridges. He was prolific, building more than 400 bridges across the US, but he always had a dream to "build the biggest thing of its kind a man could build." Strauss's company maintained a satellite office in San Francisco, and when he was contacted by Michael O'Shaughnessy about bridging the Golden Gate, Strauss was sure he had found his dream project.

Strauss submitted preliminary sketches with his estimate of $27 million.[7] On June 28, 1921, O'Shaughnessy evaluated the proposals. Strauss's proposed bridge was a giant version of his bascule drawbridges, utilitarian but ugly. But because Lindenthal's bid was way out of the ballpark and McMath did not submit one, Strauss won by default. Joseph Strauss, a 5' 3" tall bundle of energy, would spend most of the remainder of his life promoting and building the Golden Gate Bridge.

Original Strauss design rejected for aesthetic reasons

FROM DREAM TO REALITY – WINNING OVER HEARTS AND MINDS

The Golden Gate Bridge was initially opposed by powerful interests, including Southern Pacific Railroad and also by the US Department of War.[8] Southern Pacific owned the profitable Golden Gate Ferry Company, so its opposition was a foregone conclusion. That alone wasn't sufficient to stop the project, but the War Department owned the land on both sides of the bridge and also had jurisdiction over all harbor construction affecting shipping lanes. Nothing could happen without War Department support.

Faced by these powerful opponents and numerous other imposing obstacles, Strauss began crusading tirelessly to win San Francisco's hearts and minds over to his project.

As the populations of SF and Marin County grew, traffic conditions at the ferry boat docks worsened and waits became longer and longer. Strauss promoted the bridge at every opportunity, attending hundreds of dinners and meetings and speaking to any group that would listen. Strauss gradually won the support of more and more of San Francisco's shakers and movers, and in May of 1924 he got the break he needed. Assistant Secretary of War Colonel Herbert Deakyne, under heavy pressure from the City of San Francisco, finally issued preliminary approval for the land transfer subject to acceptable changes being made to the bridge plans by Strauss.[9] Secretary of War John Weeks soon thereafter issued a temporary permit for the bridge to be built, also pending the final plans.[10]

The Golden Gate Bridge and Highway District ("GGBHD") was formed in 1928 to own and manage the project, and its Directors met for the first time on January 23, 1929.[11] The GGBHD consisted of San Francisco, Marin, Sonoma, Del Norte, and parts of Mendocino and Napa counties. The GGBHD had earlier been authorized by the California Legislature specifically for the specific purpose of building and owning the bridge. At the first meeting of the GGBHD, Strauss was selected as the Chief Engineer for the bridge, and his fee was set at 4%. Strauss's role as Chief Engineer was predicated upon his submitting a new, more aesthetic design for the bridge that the GGBHD would have to approve.[12] The Board also named a Board of Engineering Consultants to work with Strauss. The Consulting engineers were Leon S. Moisseiff, Charles Alton Ellis, O.H. Amman, and Charles Derleth, Jr.[13]

Moisseff was considered an expert on wind stresses on bridges, and Ellis was Strauss Engineering Company's Design Engineer. Strauss had met Ellis in 1922 and believed he was the perfect engineer for his Golden Gate dream. Moisseff and Ellis collaborated to design a suspension bridge far more beautiful and efficient than Strauss's original.

Together they studied the complex forces and stresses that the bridge would be exposed to, and wrote fail-safe specifications for the bridges primary components. The Golden Gate would be the longest and highest suspension bridge ever built, and, more than anything else, its safety and durability would mark the triumph of mathematics over almost insoluble engineering challenges.

A WINNING DESIGN AND A REGRETTABLE CHARACTER FLAW

On March 1, 1930 Ellis returned to Chicago with the new design to complete the overall drawings, specifications, and cost estimates. Meanwhile Strauss hired a local architect, Irving Morrow, to design the architectural treatment for the bridge.[14] Morrow's contribution would be the now-famous Art Deco lines, the distinctive international orange color, and the lighting system.

Joseph Strauss   Charles Ellis

Strauss himself had little experience with or understanding of cable-suspension bridges, and accordingly had to rely heavily on Moisseff and Ellis. Unfortunately, Strauss at this point began to display a disturbing character flaw which would eventually become his undoing. Although Moisseff and Ellis were the visionaries who worked out the daunting design and engineering challenges presented by the project, Strauss was obsessed with claiming credit as the bridge's creator, and instead of praising the work of his engineers, he continually trivialized their contributions.[15]

On August 27, 1930, Strauss submitted Ellis's final plans to GGBHD and they were unanimously approved. Ellis then began the tedious job of stress analysis, making the thousands of calculations that would be required to build every single component of the bridge.[16] Ellis ultimately reduced his analysis down to the algebraic language that the engineering staff incorporated into the final design and that were used to prepare detailed specifications for all 10 construction contracts.[17] All of this was done by slide rule, working without today's computers.

Strauss became increasingly concerned that Ellis was receiving too much credit for the bridge's design, and in November, 1931, he ordered Ellis to take a vacation and turn his work over to someone else.[18] Ellis shortly thereafter received a follow-up letter from Strauss telling him not to come back at all. Unable to find steady work during the depression, and having become obsessed with the bridge, Ellis continued to work without pay, collaborating secretly with Moisseff and investing up to 70 hours per week until more than 10 volumes of engineering calculations were completed. Sadly, when the bridge was dedicated in 1937 and all the accolades were being passed out, Ellis's name was not even mentioned.[19]

 Not surprisingly, Strauss had also alienated other people during his quest to build the bridge, and his detractors blocked a proposed statue of Strauss for the bridge plaza. Ultimately, Strauss's widow funded the statue herself and had it inscribed as "The Man Who Built the Bridge," but it was located in a lightly-traveled area away from the bridge plaza.[20]

Not until 1949, when an obituary named him as the bridge's

designer, did Ellis receive just recognition for his enormous role in the design and engineering of the bridge. It is not known whether he ever saw the finished bridge, but in all the long years he labored over the numbers – he had made the bridge his own. Today most informed people regard Ellis as the real designer of the Golden Gate Bridge.

FINANCING THE DREAM IN THE GREAT DEPRESSION

There was no federal or state money available for the bridge, and after the stock market crashed on October 29, 1929, no help was available from Wall Street. With nowhere else to turn, the GGBHD decided to ask Bay Area voters to underwrite the construction of the bridge themselves by subscribing to a $35 million bond issue. The Board asked voters in all six California counties which would benefit from the bridge to vote on the bond issue. On November 4, 1930, the bond issue passed by the overwhelming vote of 145,657 to 46,954, or 76% to 24%.[20] Although some residents actually put up their homes or businesses as collateral in order to buy the bonds, California, like the country at large, was mired in depression and the bond issue was still not sold as 1932 began.

One of San Francisco's greatest civic boosters at the time was the charismatic Amadeo Peter Gianini, an Italian immigrant. Gianini opened a bank called the Bank of Italy in 1902, and, after the San Francisco earthquake, he set up temporary desks on the docks of the city and offered loans to devastated San Franciscans on the basis of "a face and a signature."[21]

In 1928, a year before the Great Depression began, Gianini bought the Bank of America and continued to help the city's hard-pressed citizens. In mid 1932, Joseph Strauss walked into Gianini's office and explained his 14-year struggle to build the bridge, knowing that if Gianini turned him down he had pretty much run out of options. As he finished his pitch, Gianini stood up and told Strauss "We need the bridge, and we'll take the bonds." B of A bought $6 million worth of bonds, and at last the project was off and running. [22]

Strauss was later quoted as having said, "It took two decades and two hundred million words to convince people the bridge was feasible."

BUILDING THE WORLD'S GREATEST BRIDGE

Eleven of the country's leading bridge engineering firms submitted proposals for building the Golden Gate. Contracts with a value of $23,844,000 were awarded in November, 1932. The largest contracts were awarded to:[23]

> McClintic-Marshall Construction Company, a subsidiary of Bethlehem Steel - $10.494 million for the steel towers and deck superstructure,
>
> John A. Roebling & Sons, builders of the Brooklyn Bridge - $5.855 million for the cabling,
>
> Pacific Bridge Company, one of the Hoover Dam's Six Companies - $2.935 million for constructing the piers on both sides of the bridge and another $555,000 for pouring the concrete roadway across the deck, and
>
> Barrett & Hilp - $1.860 million for constructing the cable anchorages on either side of the bridge.
>
> Work Force

The bridge had 10 primary contractors during construction, and some of them are no longer in business. Consequently, actual employment records are fragmentary, but those closest to the project estimated that 5,000 employees worked on the bridge.

Because the Golden Gate Bridge was built during the depths

of the Great Depression, there was no shortage of job applicants. Mary Currie was a spokeswoman for the GGBHD, and she recalls that *"getting a job on the Golden Gate Bridge was like winning the lottery. The men would line up and wait for the chance to get a job, literally hoping that one of the workers would hurt themselves so they might be the one to get the job."*[24]

Working on the Bridge – 750' above the bay

The working conditions, both above and below the water, were brutal. Slim Lambert, a cowboy from Washington State, recalled that *"Things were a lot different in those days. You hardly ever slowed down to a trot. If you went to the restroom and stayed more than 30 seconds the boss would come and see what was wrong with you. Lots of men were fired right on the spot, if the boss thought they were malingering a little bit. There was plenty of other men waiting right there for your job."*

On the bridge's towers, where both temperatures and winds were often in the 40s, workers stuffed newspapers into their jackets trying to keep warm. Martin Adams from Arkansas called the bridge the coldest place he had ever worked. *"You put all the clothes on you had and worked as hard as you could, or you would freeze."*

Later, after the bridge was built, Bridge spokeswoman Mary Currie said that *"workers on the bridge didn't fear death, they expected it."*[25] Despite the conditions and the nature of the work, only eleven men died working on the bridge, ten of them in one accident only two months prior to the bridge's completion.

The work on the bridge would go on for four years and four months, and it can be divided into four distinct phases.

Concrete Piers and Steel Bridge Towers

The steel sections for the two bridge towers were fabricated by Bethlehem Steel Corporation at its Pottstown, PA plant and were shipped by rail to Philadelphia, and then by boat through the Panama Canal and then up the Pacific Coast to the Bay Area.

While the towers were en route the two bridge piers were being laid. The north pier on the Marin side was placed on the shoreline, and it was relatively simple and straightforward. It rested on bedrock 20' below the surface of the water. The Marin pier required 47,000 tons of concrete, into which steel base slabs were set. Cranes then lifted the steel tower sections, which were riveted atop each other as the tower rose. Each tower contained 600,000 rivets. The Marin tower was completed in October of 1934.

The San Francisco tower was a completely different story. The pier for the south tower was placed in 100 feet of water 1,100 feet from the shore, and was the first bridge pier ever sunk in an open ocean.[26] Consequently, there was no precedent in civil engineering for many of the problems encountered during its construction. The pier was reached by an 1,100 foot "access trestle." To protect the pier from a fog bound ship, Pacific Bridge lowered 30' thick concrete slabs into the ocean to create an enclosure called a "fender" which was the size of a football field with rounded corners. Divers then descended inside the fender to position blasting tubes and guide panels and beams into proper position. Much of the time the divers worked blindly, forced to feel their way along by the murky water and the cumbersome diving suits.[27] The blasting tubes were filled with black powder explosive to blast the bedrock for the tower foundations. Due to constantly changing tides and currents, divers could only submerge for four, 24 minute periods each day, and they worked knowing full well that the fender walls might collapse at any time from the intense pressure of the currents. [28]

The San Francisco tower pier surrounded by its fender – 1935

When the divers finished their work in December, 1934, workers pumped an estimated 9.7 million gallons of water out of the fender, leaving it dry for the pouring of the foundation. Three hundred sixty-four thousand tons of concrete were then poured into the fender to form the foundation for the tower. The San Francisco tower was completed in June, 1935, and then the 10 million gallons of water were pumped back into the fender.

The two towers rise 746' above the water and 500' above the road way, and each one weighs 44,000 tons. In the 1930s, they were easily the tallest towers ever built.[29]

Cable Anchorages

The bridge would have two huge main cables which would pass over the two towers, resting in "saddles" on the tops of each one, and anchored in giant concrete foundations at either end. Cables are subject to "tension" which is a function of many variables, including primarily the weight they support adjusted for winds and temperatures. Moisseff and Ellis determined that the cables would each be 7,650 feet long, that their diameters would be 36.375," and each one would weigh 11,000 tons. They wanted the bridge to have maximum transverse deflection at its center point of 27.7 feet, meaning that they wanted it to be able to swing longitudinally by up to almost 28' in high winds.[30]

Using these constants, and working only with slide rules, they were able to calculate that each of the four cable anchorages would require 60,000 tons of concrete. Workers excavated an estimated 3.25 million cubic feet of dirt on both sides of the bridge to accommodate the pylons and anchorages. This work, described as being similar to building a stadium, was begun 1933 and completed in 1936. The anchorage construction marked the first time that rotating drum concrete mixers, which are commonplace today, were ever used.

Spinning the Cables

Perhaps the most remarkable of all the engineering innovations that were introduced during the bridge's construction was the technique used to construct the main cables, then the largest in the world.

John Roebling and Sons, the world-renowned builders of cable-based suspension bridges, had been awarded the cable contract for the Golden Gate Bridge. Fifty-two years earlier, the same Company had built the Brooklyn Bridge. Its engineers had devised the world's most efficient strength-to-rigidity ratio for cables, and had also developed a technique for "spinning" cables on site and in place. A fixture within the anchorage called a "strand shoe" was used to secure a wire (the "dead" wire") while a spinning wheel (aka a "Sheave") pulled the wire across the bridge. When it reached the other side, the wire was secured to that strand shoe, and the wheel then returned with a new wire (the "live wire") which it looped around (spun) the dead wire. The sheave continued to spin the wires back and forth across the mile long plus bridge until the target number of wires had been spun.[31]

Each of the special purpose wires was cold-drawn and double galvanized. Each wire was .192" in diameter, about the circumference of a wooden pencil. The wires were flexible over long lengths, but each was so strong that an 18" length could not be bent by hand.[32] Each Golden Gate bridge main cable contained 27,572 individual wires, so the spinning wheel had to make the crossing 27,572 times for each cable. Laid end to end, the wires were 80,000 miles long. Their contract gave Roebling and Sons fourteen months to spin the 80,000 miles of wire into two giant main cables. To ensure they made the deadline, the Roebling engineers designed a "split tram," a second spinning wheel which met the first wheel in the middle of the bridge, essentially doubling the speed. Eventually, they came up with a system that was able to spin six wires simultaneously – color coded to prevent confusion. Using the new system, Roebling could spin as much as 1,000 miles of wire across the bridge in an 8 hour shift, and in good weather, the wheels could travel half way across the span in just six minutes.[33] Their "on-the-job" engineering innovations, particularly the split trams, enabled Roebling to complete the cable spinning in just six months and nine days, an incredible eight months ahead of schedule.[34] The cable spinning officially ended on May 20, 1936.

Roebling on the tower with cable spinners – 1935

The finished cables were each 36.375 inches in diameter, and 7,650 feet long. Each cable weighed approximately 11,000 tons.

Suspender Ropes and Suspended Deck Spans

Main cable bands are located at 50' intervals on the main cables on both sides of the Bridge. Pairs of verticle cable "suspender ropes" (actually steel cables) are hung from the cable bands. Each suspender rope has a diameter of 2.6875". The purpose of the suspender ropes is to support the three roadway spans of the bridge. The bridge has 250 pairs of suspender ropes.[35]

The last major step in building the bridge was the installation of the three suspended steel roadway spans and the 7" concrete deck, which began in June, 1936. More than any other phase of construction, progress on the deck was in full display to observers, and anyone watching could see the sections grow closer and closer to each other every day. The finished length of the main suspended span was 4,200 feet (the distance between the two towers), and each of the two side spans were 1,125 feet long, giving the combined spans of the bridge a total length of 6,450 feet. The total weight of the suspended deck with the road surface was about 154,000 tons.[36]

The width of the bridge is 90 feet. The width of the roadway between curbs is 62 feet, and the width of the sidewalk is 10 feet. The clearance above the water at high tide is 220 feet. The spans were joined and the concrete deck was poured in November of 1936.

Finished at Last

The bridge was completed on April 19, 1937, $1.3 million under budget and ahead of schedule, due almost entirely to Roebling's cable spinning innovations developed on site.

A bridge grand-opening celebration began on May 27, 1937. Before it was opened to traffic, 200,000 people crossed the bridge on foot or roller skates. Strauss wrote an

Opening Day on the Bridge – May 27, 1937

original poem commemorating the bridge entitled "The

Mighty Task is Done." Strauss officially presented the completed bridge to the GGTBHD.[37]

Strauss was paid $1 million and a given a lifetime bridge pass for his work.[38]

POST- CONSTRUCTION ECONOMICS

Since it opened the GGB has carried average daily traffic of 110,000 cars.[39] The toll structure divides traffic into several levels and categories and is quite complicated, but based upon today's toll structure the bridge probably generates in the neighborhood of $250,000 each day, which is about $90 million annually. The bond issue was retired on schedule in 1971 entirely out of tolls and the bridge has been a financial success.[40] With its graceful cables, its beautiful color and its magnificent backdrop, the Golden Gate Bridge continues to be regarded by many as one of the world's most beautiful man-made structures.

LASTING CULTURAL LEGACY

Joseph Bearman Strauss devoted sixteen years of his life to the Golden Gate Bridge, and his career dream was to be known to posterity as "the man who built the Golden Gate Bridge." Unfortunately for Strauss, his obsession with claiming all credit as the Bridge's creator was to become his undoing. His habit of minimizing the contributions of Charles Ellis and Leon Moisseff alienated many important figures, and these detractors ultimately blocked the commemorative statue that Strauss had planned for himself on the bridge plaza.

In the years that have passed since the bridge's completion, engineers who have studied the project have tended to give more credit to Ellis and Moisseff and less to Strauss. Strauss was undoubtedly the driving force behind the bridge and was a superb promoter and construction superintendant, but in reality he probably had little to do with either designing the bridge or overcoming its daunting engineering challenges. Legend has it that Moisseff and Ellis designed the Golden Gate Bridge to withstand a 90 mph wind, bumper to bumper traffic both ways, a tidal surge of 4.6 million feet per second, and an 8.8 earthquake – all at the same time.

Ironically, had Strauss been willing to give his two exceptional engineers their just due, his own role in the project would likely have been enhanced rather than diminished. Joseph Strauss died of a stroke less than a year after the bridge opened to public on May 27, 1937.[41] Leon Moisseff died in 1943. Charles Ellis lived until 1949, and his obituary named him the Designer of the Golden Gate Bridge.[42] It is not known whether he ever saw or stood on the finished bridge.

Notwithstanding the contributions of its creators, the Golden Gate Bridge has become a great cultural icon, and is known and revered world-wide. Few visitors to San Francisco leave the city without having ridden a cable car and crossed the Golden Gate Bridge.

The American Society of Civil Engineers ("ASCE") is the oldest national engineering society in the United States, and it claims more than 140,000 members world-wide. In 1994, "as a tribute to modern society's ability to achieve the unachievable, reach unreachable heights, and scorn the notion of 'it can't be done,'" the ASCE sought nominations from all its members around the globe for the Seven Wonders of the Modern World. The chosen projects pay tribute to the seven, greatest civil engineering achievements of the 20th century.

The Golden Gate Bridge was one of the projects chosen.[43]

CHAPTER 3

MANHATTAN SKYSCRAPERS & THE EMPIRE STATE BUILDING

A BRIEF HISTORY OF MANHATTAN SKYSCRAPERS

The development of steel-frame construction and the advent of the elevator in the late 1800s made the construction of tall buildings possible, but existing building codes would have to be changed in most cities before they could become reality.[1] In 1892 New York City eliminated a provision in its building code that required that masonry be used for fireproofing considerations.[2] This change paved the way for steel-skeleton construction, and left the development of skyscraper technology as the only obstacle to redrawing the Manhattan skyline.

In 1897 a young architect in Chicago named Paul Starrett went to work for the George

A. Fuller Construction Company and in 1900 he was transferred to New York City, where Fuller had had just moved its home offices.[3] Starrett would manage the construction of the Flatiron Building, which would become New York's second skyscraper. The Flatiron's architect was Craig Burnham, Starrett's former employer in Chicago, and since Burnham's design employed a steel skeleton, the Flatiron could theoretically be built to 22 stories. With Starrett and Burnham working together, the Flatiron Building topped out in 1902 at 307 feet, and Starrett, 36 years old at the time, would go on to become the foremost builder of skyscrapers in the world.

In 1908 the Singer Tower, at 612 feet with 47 floors, became Manhattan's and the world's tallest building. It wore the crown for only one year, until it was surpassed by the Met Life Tower at 700 feet and 50 floors. The F.W. Woolworth Building was completed in 1913, and its 57 floors rose to a height of 792 feet.[4]

World War I broke out in 1914, and when it ended in 1918 the United States fell into a mild depression. These events created a lull in the tall building boom which enabled the Woolworth Building to hold the crown of "world's tallest building" for 17 years until 1930, when the now-fabled "Race to the Top" would end its reign.

THE ROARING TWENTIES

Business-friendly Republican Warren G. Harding became President in 1921, and in a short time the recession was over and a period of unprecedented growth and prosperity began. The decade of the Twenties marked the introduction of electricity, telephones, automobiles, and motion pictures, all of which created major changes in American life styles and standards of living. Athletes and movie stars were becoming national celebrities, and giant sports stadiums and beautiful theatres were springing up everywhere. In 1927 Babe Ruth hit 60 home runs and became the King of the New York City. It was the decade of jazz music, speakeasies, Art Deco, flappers, and unbridled optimism.

Woolworth Building nearing completion - 1913

The 57-story Woolworth Building was still the world's tallest building as it had been since 1913. But in 1928 the Manhattan skyline began to change dramatically, and in less than three years, the Woolworth Building would be dwarfed by three new giants. In 1931 the 102-story Empire State Building would be wearing the crown of world's tallest building.

THE RACE TO THE TOP

Urbanization had reached a climax in the US during the Roaring Twenties, and for the first time more Americans lived in large cities than in small towns or rural areas. The nation had become fascinated with its great metropolitan centers (they were home to about 15% of the population), and the new fascination created a building boom in the cities.[5] New York City was rapidly becoming the world's financial center, and was suddenly experiencing a serious shortage of downtown office space. An architectural battle was heating up, and by the beginning of 1929, three projects in Manhattan were competing furiously not only to cure the shortage but also to wear the crown of world's tallest building.

MANHATTAN SKYSCRAPERS

40 WALL STREET

The 40 Wall Street Corporation was formed in 1929 to build a speculative skyscraper for an anchor tenant, the Manhattan Company (forerunner to Chase Manhattan Bank).[6] The developer was investment banker George Ohrstrom, known on Wall Street as "the kid." The principal architect for the building was H. Craig Severance, and the consulting architects were Shreve, Lamb, and Harmon. Among the principal owners of 40 Wall Street were Paul Starrett and his newly formed Company Starrett Brothers and Eken, who were also its general contractors.[7] Severance, the building's architect, was a former partner of William Van Alen, who was the principal architect of the Chrysler Building (see below), which was being designed and built at the same time.

40 Wall Street's original plan for the building called for a modest 47 stories. But then the team learned of plans for the competing Chrysler Building and a series of upward revisions began. The plan was first amended to 60 stories, and it was then raised to 67 stories and 840 feet, which Severance believed was sufficient to eclipse both the Woolworth Building and the Chrysler Building. When Severance and Starrett learned at the last minute that the rival Chrysler Building was going to 925 feet, they amended their plans once more to top out at 927 feet and 72 stories.[8]

Ground was broken in May 1929, and Starrett devised an ingenious way of laying of new foundation footers while he was still demolishing the old ones.[9] The foundations were ready in just three weeks, giving 40 Wall Street a jump on the Chrysler Building, and the entire steel frame for the 72 story building was completed in just 93 days, on September 2.[10] This astonishing pace was a tribute to Starrett, who would display his organizational genius many more times on this and other projects. By early-April, 1929, the building was topped out at 927 feet, and it was ready for occupancy on schedule on May 1. For a period of slightly less than one month, 40 Wall Street (aka "The Manhattan Building") was the world's tallest building. The all-in construction cost was $13,091,416 and construction was completed in 12 months.[11]

Despite financial difficulties which would plague it, the building became widely known as "The Crown Jewel of Wall Street," and in 1932 W. Parker Chase wrote of the building:

> *"This marvelous example of architectural and building skill is not only a credit to New York, but to all America.*
>
> *No building ever constructed more thoroughly typifies the American spirit of hustle than does this extraordinary structure - <u>built in less than one year.</u> Words are inadequate to convey even a faint conception of the splendor or the wonder of this magnificent building."* [12]

THE CHRYSLER BUILDING

The story of the Chrysler Building began in early 1928. The site was owned by former New York State Senator William H. Reynolds. Reynolds wanted to build a 67 story building office building at 405 Lexington Avenue that would surpass the Woolworth Building as the world's tallest. He hired architect William Van Alen to design the building for him. When the architectural drawings were almost completed Reynolds decided the plan was too expensive, and he sold the entire project, including an 84 year land lease and the architectural drawings, to Walter P. Chrysler, who wanted to move his Company's headquarters from Detroit to New York City. Chrysler paid Reynolds $2 million for the package, and the race was on.[13]

Walter Chrysler knew about 40 Wall Street, and he wanted his building to be both taller and first. Because his building was already permitted and designed, Chrysler decided to keep Van Alen as his architect to save time and avoid starting over. He would work closely with Van Alen to add additional floors and the now-famous ornamental features copied from Chrysler automobiles. Chrysler hired Ralph Squire & Sons as his structural engineers.

Ground was broken for what would become the Chrysler Building, located at 405 Lexington Avenue, on September 19, 1928, well ahead of 40 Wall Street, but extensive revisions to the building's plan slowed things down, and Chrysler did not have the benefit of Starrett's engineering genius. The Chrysler Building was built to become the headquarters for the Chrysler Corporation, but it was designed and paid for by Walter P. Chrysler personally.[14]

According to Van Alen's revised design for Chrysler, the building's height was to be 860 feet, and it was to contain 71 floors. But in April, 1929, 40 Wall Street announced a revised target height of 925 feet, and Chrysler immediately ordered Van Alen to add 6 more floors and 65 feet to his building, making it exactly the same height as 40 Wall Street. Learning of this, Severance increased the height of his 40 Wall Street Building by 2 more feet in order to claim the title, but Chrysler still had one more card to play.

He had asked Van Alen to construct a 121-foot-tall spire inside the frame of the Chrysler Building, swearing everyone on his team to secrecy. After 40 Wall Street was completed on April 30, 1930, topping out at 927 feet, Van Alen quietly and without fanfare added his spire, bringing the Chrysler Building to 1,046 feet, not only surpassing 40 Wall but also enabling it to pass the Eiffel Tower as the world's tallest man-made structure.[15]

The story did not have a happy ending for Van Alen. Walter Chrysler claimed that Van Alen had accepted bribes from his sub contractors and refused to pay him his architectural fee. Van Alen ultimately won a judgement against Chrysler, but it is not known whether he was ever paid. Notwithstanding, his reputation was irreparably damaged, and even though Van Alen was only 47 years old, he never won another major architectural commission.[16]

The Chrysler Building's best-known features are the seven, distinctive, radiating stainless steel arches at its top, and the replicas of 1929 Chrysler hood ornaments and radiator caps on the corners of the 31st and 61st floors.[17]

Chrysler hood ornament – 61st floor

The Chrysler Building would hold the record for world's tallest for less than one year, when the Empire State Building would take it away, but it remains one of the world's most famous buildings and its best-loved examples of the Art Deco architectural style.

THE EMPIRE STATE BUILDING

The man who built the ESB was John Jakob Raskob. In 1901 he became personal secretary to Pierre S. duPont, and Raskob remained a close business associate and confidante of duPont and the duPont family throughout his life.[18] Raskob also had been an early investor in General Motors, and he helped the duPonts engineer their acquisition of a 43% ownership interest in GM from the Company's Founder, William Durant.[19]

During the 1920s Raskob lived in Detroit and simultaneously held the positions of Vice President and Chief Financial Officer for both General Motors and E.I.duPont de Nemours and Company, two of the world's largest companies. Raskob was a strong supporter of Al Smith in the 1928 Presidential Election, and in that year he became Chairman of the Democratic National Committee.[20] Alfred P. Sloan, GM's President at the time, was a supporter of Republican candidate Herbert Hoover, and Sloan asked Raskob to resign either from GM or the RNC.

Raskob, then 49 years old, decided to resign from GM, sold his GM stock, and set out for New York to build the Empire State Building. He quickly assembled a group of well known investors and formed Empire State, Inc. The investors were Coleman duPont, Pierre duPont, Louis G. Kaufman and Ellis P. Earl. He appointed Alfred E. Smith, former Governor of New York who had just lost the 1928 Presidential election to Herbert Hoover, as President of Empire State, Inc.[21] Now all Raskob needed was a site.

Pierre DuPont & John Raskob

In mid-town Manhattan the original Waldorf Astoria Hotel had occupied the intersection of 5th Avenue and West 34th Street since 1893, but by 1928 the elegant social life of New York upon which its success depended had moved farther north. The Astor family closed the old hotel on May 3, 1929, and began work on a new one on 50th street. The Astors sold the 34th Street property to Empire State, Inc., for $15 million, and Raskob was ready to go. [22]

ASSEMBLING THE TEAM

Raskob chose Shreve, Lamb, and Harmon Associates as his architects. The three were known as the best skyscraper designers in the city. Raskob was particularly interested in Partner William Lamb, a graduate of Williams College and Columbia School of Architecture. Lamb was only 35 years old, and relished the opportunity. Raskob reportedly told Lamb that he not only wanted the tallest office building in New York, but he also wanted it finished first. [23]

The architects created a design with four facades facing the street, instead of the customary one. The building's highlight would be its imperious tower. This was a simple, but adventurous design and the project also had an adventurous schedule – it had to be completed in 18 months. Starrett Brothers and Eken, the premier skyscraper builders of the 1920s, were bidders for the General Contractor spot. Paul Starrett was then 65 years old, and as noted above had built a reputation as an innovator and an organizational genius. Among his credits were Penn Station, the Flatiron Building, the Plaza Hotel, and the Lincoln Memorial, and he just finishing his work on 40 Wall Street. Starrett made a bold and innovative bid to win the ESB job. The modus operandi of the day for contractors was to rent the necessary construction equipment for each project and then to charge the project for the rent. Because this project required so much specialized equipment that was unique to ESB, Starrett proposed to have the equipment built to spec. Empire State, Inc. would own it. When the building was completed Starrett would sell equipment and credit the project for the proceeds. Starrett also proposed to employ Homer Gage Balcom, the country's foremost expert on the effects of lateral wind forces on buildings, as their Structural Engineer. Starrett Bros and Eken won the job.[24]

The peak workforce during construction was 3,500, including 328 arch laborers, 290 bricklayers, 384 brick laborers, 225 carpenters, 107 derrick operators, 105 electricians, 249 elevator installers, 194 HVAC installers, 192 plumbers, 285 steelworkers (most of them famed Mohawk "high steel walkers") plus clerks, foremen, inspectors, water boys, and a number of other specialists.[25] The workforce invested more than seven million man hours in the job, and weekly payrolls at peak times approached $250,000. The men often worked around the clock in shifts, and concessionaires operated restaurants on various floors so workers did not have to descend to street level for their meals.[26]

THE ICONIC STRUCTURE RISES

The overall design of the project was driven entirely by Raskob's insistence that the building be completed by May 1, 1931. The Race to the Top with Chrysler and 40 Wall Street was not the only factor influencing Raskob. He was taking a calculated financial gamble. None of the more than 2 million square feet of office space was leased ahead of time. Raskob was gambling that tenants would line up to work in the world's tallest and most famous building, but he also knew they wouldn't wait forever. He was pretty sure that if he couldn't open in 1931, 40 Wall Street and the Chrysler would already have gobbled up all the choice prospective tenants. According to commercial real estate practices of the time, lease agreements were written with annual terms that always began on May 1, meaning that if the building was not ready for occupancy by that date, the Lessor would lose an entire year's rent on the space.[27] His schedule simply had to be met.

Raskob was a seasoned financial executive who adhered religiously to the principle that time was money, and he believed the construction process could be automated just like the process for building automobiles. The stakeholders in the ESB adopted a team approach that required close collaboration and constant communication among the owners, architects, engineers, and contractors on a daily basis throughout the whole project.

The first 85 floors of the Empire State Building were designed as rentable office space, and these floors lent themselves well to Raskob's "assembly line" construction concept. Floors 86 through 102, on the other hand, were unique to the Empire State Building, being reserved for an iconic glass, steel and concrete art deco spire with two observation decks.

Starrett Bros & Eken employed a brand new concept called "fast-track construction" to construct the first 85 floors, and devised many innovative construction methods and techniques on the fly as the work progressed.[28]

The first challenge was excavating for the foundations. Demolition of the old Waldorf Astoria had begun on October 1, and was scheduled to take several months. Starrett Bros. had pioneered a method of simultaneous demolition and excavation on their own building at 40 Wall a year earlier, and he was able to devise a way to do it once again at ESB.[29] Excavation began ahead of schedule in January, 1930, and two shifts of 300 men each worked around the clock to dig through the hard rock creating the foundation footings. The footings were completed on March 1, 1930, giving the team exactly fourteen months to have the building ready for occupancy. Out of deference to his old Irish friend and now Company President Al Smith, Raskob celebrated the laying of the first steel on St. Patrick's Day, 1930, with a formal ribbon cutting ceremony.[30]

The building at two stories – April, 1930

Logistics presented the next big challenge to the team. The building site was surrounded on all sides by other buildings, so there was very little storage space available for construction materials and supplies. Accordingly, sub-contractors were required to do most of their fabrication and sub-assembly work off-site, and just-in-time deliveries had to be scheduled literally down to the minute. It was said that the flow of materials to the plant was so efficient that everything delivered to the site was in the building in less than three days, and that steel beams arrived from the forging plants too hot to touch with bare hands.[31]

A second logistical challenge to Starrett was presented by material handling, and the smooth and safe movement of tools and equipment up and down the structure's more than 100 floors. He configured the site to contain 11 derricks, 17 hoists, and two concrete plants. All steel beams and posts had to arrive at the site already coded with both their locations in the framework, and number of the derrick that would lift them into place. Starrett's carefully designed system often enabled steelworkers to have beams riveted in place within 80 hours after they left the steel forges.

The traditional method of transporting bricks and small tools around construction sites was to use wheelbarrows. There were 10 million bricks in the ESB, however, and moving them by wheelbarrow would be inefficient and impractical. Starrett devised a system of narrow-gauge railway tracks and railway carts to replace wheelbarrows. The tracks were installed in a loop on each floor, and each cart carried 8 times the load of a wheelbarrow.[32] When bricks arrived at the site they were fed down a chute into a hopper in the basement. When they were needed the bricks would be loaded into a railway car and the car would be hoisted to the appropriate floor, where the narrow-gauge tracks would take them to their final destination.

Hoisting a steel beam - 1931

Starrett's innovations revolutionized the construction of tall buildings, and represented a triumph of his engineering genius. In the eight month period March through October, 1930, he completed the first 85 floors of the Empire State Building and it eclipsed the Chrysler Building as the world's tallest. This meant that Starrett Brothers & Eken had built the equivalent of world's tallest building from groundbreaking to completion in an astonishing 300 days.

But work on the Empire state Building was not finished. The 85th floor of the building was the highest floor used for rentable office space, and after completing that floor Starrett Brothers went to work on the observation decks, the mooring mast and the spire.[33] Observation decks were constructed on both the 86th and 102nd floors. The portion of the tower between the 86th and 102nd floors was originally intended as a mooring mast for blimps and airships, but actually ended up as the base for a broadcast antenna. The antenna was added to the top of the spire in the early 1950s to transmit the broadcast signals of several television and FM stations. On the

102nd floor there is a door with stairs ascending up to the 103rd floor. The 103rd floor was originally a landing platform for dirigibles, but the stairs and a ladder now lead to the antenna for maintenance work.

Although NBC initially had the exclusive rights to the transmission antenna, today the signals of more than 50 television and radio stations are transmitted from it.[34]

THE BUILDING IS COMPLETED – AHEAD OF SCHEDULE IN RECORD TIME

The construction of the Empire State Building was completed on April 11, 1931, 391 days after the ribbon-cutting and only 444 days after ground-breaking The Building came in ahead of schedule and under budget, primarily as the result of teamwork and brilliant organizational skills. Starrett's meticulous planning, streamlined logistics, innovative construction techniques and a skilled and dedicated workforce enabled the team to raise the steel framework of the ESB at the astonishing rate of 4½ stories per week, a rate that has never been equaled before or since by any comparable structure.[35]

The Empire State Building is 424 feet long and 187 feet wide, making a footprint of approximately 2 acres. It has 102 floors, the top floor reaching 1,250 feet high. The tip of its antenna reaches 1,454 feet.

The completed Empire State Building included:

- 10 million bricks,

- 57,000 tons of steel,

- 62,000 cubic yards of concrete,

- 200,000 cubic feet of Indiana limestone,

- 310,000 square feet of Hauteville and Rocheron marble,

- 70 miles of water mains,

- 2.5 million feet of electrical wire,

- 1,000 miles of telephone cable, and

- 73 elevators [36]

The building contains 2.1 million square feet of usable office space, and it boasts its own zip code - 10118.

POST-CONSTRUCTION ECONOMICS

All three buildings were conceived in the best of times and completed in the worst. There has probably never been a time in American history where fortunes went from boom to bust so quickly. The developers of two of the three buildings regarded their projects as "speculations" from the outset, but they could not possibly have foreseen the devastating financial outcomes for their projects. Walter Chrysler was probably always reasonably confident in his investment because his own Company was his largest tenant, but 40 Wall Street and Empire State, Inc. had no safety net.

40 Wall Street

Two basements and the first six floors were designed specifically for a bank tenant, and Bank of Manhattan occupied this space from the time the building opened until 1960, when it became Chase Manhattan Bank and opened its own headquarters building.[37] But the bank floors in total represented only about ⅛ of the total available space. From its inception 40 Wall Street had been a "speculative skyscraper," and its financial success was dependent upon continuation of the booming, but underserved commercial real estate market that existed in Manhattan in 1928. The stock market crashed in October, 1929, six months after the building's Grand Opening, and many of the companies who had leased space for $8 per square foot were bankrupt by 1930. The Great Depression persisted, and 40 Wall Street struggled to find tenants and meet payments for the next ten years until August of 1940, when Marine Midland Bank, acting as Trustee for the building's bondholders, foreclosed on the property.[38]

Marine Midland formed a shell Company called 40 Wall Street Building, Inc., to own the building, and purchased it for $11,500,000, the exact amount of the Bond Issue.[39] Holders of a second mortgage, preferred stock, and common stock (most of which were Starrett Bros. interests) were financially wiped out and received nothing.[40]

In 1944 as the War wound down and the country recovered from the Great Depression, 40 Wall Street was fully leased for the first time. The building cash-flowed for most of the next 45 years, and when the Bank of Manhattan left in 1960, Manufacturers' Hanover took the bank floors and stayed for another thirty years.

On the evening of May 20, 1946, a United States Air Force C-45 Beechcraft airplane crashed into the north side of 40 Wall Street. It struck the 58th floor of the building at about 8:10 PM, creating a 20 by 10-foot (3.0 m) hole in the masonry, and killing all five aboard the plane, including a WAC officer.[41] Parts of the aircraft and pieces of brick and mortar from the building fell into the street below, but there were no reported injuries to any of the estimated 2,000 workers in the building, nor anyone on the street.

In 1988 the building was purchased by developer Jack Resnick, who had big plans for improvements and renovations. Unfortunately the building was falling into disrepair, and its largest tenant, Manufacturers' Hanover, left in 1990. In 1992, Cushman & Wakefield's records showed that 585,000 square feet of floor space, or over half the building, was vacant.[42]

In 1995 Donald Trump bought 40 Wall Street for $8 million, which was $5 million less than its original cost. Trump thoroughly renovated and updated the building, and it has been profitable ever since.[43]

The Chrysler Building

The Chrysler Building has enjoyed pretty much uninterrupted profitability since it was completed. From 1930 to the mid-1950s the building served as headquarters for the Chrysler Corporation. Walter P. Chrysler died in 1940, and in 1953 the Chrysler family sold the building to William Zeckendorf. In 1957 Zeckendorf sold the Chrysler Building to investors Sol Goldman and Alex DiLorenzo, who in turn sold it to Massachusetts Mutual Life Insurance Company.

Jack Kent Cooke, one-time owner of both the Washington Redskins and the Los Angeles Lakers, owned the Building from 1979 until he died in 1997.[44] Mr. Cooke's estate sold the building to Tishman Speyer Properties and the Traveler's Insurance Group, reportedly for $220 million. A 75% ownership stake in the Chrysler Building was purchased by the German Investment Group TMW for $300 million in 2001, and in 2008 Abu Dhabi Investment Council, the present owner, acquired a 90% ownership stake in the Chrysler Building and a smaller neighboring property for $800 million.

The Empire State Building

When the building opened in May, 1931, the United States was already deep into the Great Depression. The tenants who Raskob had hoped would line up at his door were instead downsizing and looking for lower cost space. In its first full year of operation, visits to the observation decks were the Empire State Building's largest source of revenue.[45] In 1933 fifty-six floors were vacant, and New Yorkers referred to the ESB as the "The Empty State Building."[46] In addition to the Depression, the ESB was hampered by its location, which was not very close to either Grand Central or Penn Station.

On the morning of Saturday, July 28, 1945, a B-25 pilot flying his plane toward Newark Airport got lost in fog and crashed into the 78th and 79th floors of the Empire State Building. The resulting explosion killed the plane's crew and several volunteers, who were working on the building that day. As a testament to the building's structural strength, damage was limited and the building was open the next day.[47] Elevator service was restored within weeks of the accident, and the building was fully restored at a cost of $1 million.

The Empire State Building lost money until the economy recovered in the post war years. It first posted a profit in 1950, which was ironically the year that its visionary and majority owner John Jacob Raskob died. In 1951 the Raskob estate sold the building to Roger L. Stevens and Henry J. Crown for $51 million, which was at the time the largest price ever paid for a single piece of real estate.[48] By that time occupancy had risen to above 95%, where it stayed thereafter. Colonel Henry Crown bought Stevens out in 1954, and in 1961 he sold the building for $65 million to a syndicate including Harry B. Helmsley, Lawrence A. Wien, and Wien's son-in-law Peter Malkin. The syndicate sold the land under the building to Prudential Insurance for $29 million.

In 1991 Prudential sold the land for $42 million to a party secretly representing Hideki Yokoi, then serving a prison sentence for arson, which set off a seven-year legal battle between Yokoi and the Helmsley/Malkin syndicate. In 2002 Yokoi sold the land to a partnership set up by Malkin, and Malkin and his son-in-law ultimately wrested control of the building from the Helmsley estate.

In 2008 Malkin's partnership "Empire State Building Associates" announced a $550 million upgrade of the building, and in 2013 ESBA formed a $5.2 billion publicly traded Real Estate Investment Trust to own and manage the ESB and 16 other properties.[49]

LASTING CULTURAL LEGACY

Although none of the three buildings holds the title of world's tallest any longer, all three remain crowning engineering marvels and they represent amazing accomplishments in the field of commercial construction. All three buildings were built from start to finish in the astonishingly short time of 12 months, give or take a few days. Certainly quality was not sacrificed for speed. All three are not only still standing 85 years later, but they are still among the most sought-after addresses in Manhattan.

The Trump Building (formerly 40 Wall Street) is still the "Crown Jewel of Wall Street," and the Chrysler Building remains perhaps the world's most admired example of Art Deco architecture.

The Empire State Building today is home to 1,000 tenants, and 21,000 people work there every day. Its seventy-three elevators will get you from street level to the 80th floor in 1 minute.[50] The building's three-story main lobby was restored to its original look in 2009, and, as a testament to Starrett's original construction team, the lobby restoration took longer and cost more than it had taken to build the entire building 78 years earlier.[51]

Empire State Building at twilight

In 1955, the Empire State Building was named as one the Seven Greatest American Engineering Achievements of All Time by the American Society of Civil Engineers ("ASCE").[52] In 1996 it was selected by ASCE as one of the "Seven Wonders of the Modern World," and in 2001 the engineering society named it one of only 10 "Monuments of the Millenium." Its observation decks are still visited by millions of people every year.

The speed with which these structures were built still puzzles today's architects and contractors, and it begs the question – why could those men in 1930, in the depths of a great depression and with technology and equipment that was primitive by today's standards, build their great buildings several times faster than anyone has ever been able to build one since?

Is it possible that the decline of America is mirrored in the construction of its greatest engineering marvels?

We have compiled a list of comparable projects completed in the United States since 1950 with construction times noted. Our list is below. Without exception it has taken at least two times and as many eight times longer to build all these structures than it took the men in New York City 85 years ago.

TEN TALLEST BUILDINGS IN USA – 2015

Rank	Building Name	City	Year Comp.	Days To Build
1	One World Trade Center	New York City	2014	3,165*
2	Sears (Now Willis) Tower	Chicago	1974	1,035
3	432 Park Avenue	New York City	2014	1,200
4	Trump Int'l Hotel & Tower	Chicago	2009	1,245
5	World Trade Center (2)**	New York City	1972	885
6	Empire State Building	New York City	1931	404
7	Bank of America Tower	New York City	2009	1,600
8	Standard Oil (now Aon) Center	Chicago	1973	1,365
9	John Hancock Building	Chicago	1969	1,460
10	Chrysler Building	New York City	1930	600

Days during which the site was shut down by Court order not included

** *Destroyed by terrorists in 2001*

CHAPTER 4

THE PENTAGON

THE GATHERING STORM

The title of the first volume of Churchill's epic "The Second World War" perfectly describes the situation that existed in the US War Department in early 1941. Both Secretary of War Henry Stimson and Army Chief of Staff George Marshall knew it would only be a short time before the United States would be drawn into the war.

General Marshall and Secretary of War Stimson

Japan was at war with China, France had surrendered, Germany, Japan, and Italy had formed the Axis, and the Nazis had just invaded Russia with 3 million soldiers. On May 27 President Roosevelt had declared a national emergency,[1] and an unprecedented troop mobilization had already begun. The country's military personnel count would increase by almost four times from 458,000 in 1940 to 1,800,000 in 1941, and would ultimately reach 12 million at the height of the war.

The Construction Division of the Army Quartermaster Corps was charged with building camps to house and train the new recruits, and its budget had recently been increased from $10 million to more than $70 million a month.[2] The Construction Division was swamped with orders to build camps, munitions plants, housing projects, and airfields, and its offices were teeming with salesman, contractors, and equipment vendors. It soon became obvious to both Stimson and Marshall that their Construction Division could not keep pace with demands, and they decided they quickly had to find someone with the "necessary drive" to run the entire program.

General Marshall gave the Secretary the name of a dynamic lieutenant-colonel in the Army Corps of Engineers. His name was Brehon Burke Somervell.

THE DRIVING FORCE

Brehon Burke Somervell had graduated sixth in his class at West Point in 1914. It was said that he excelled in everything he did. He was a superb marksman and rider, and a star fencer. His classmates envied him for his elegant good looks.[3] Upon graduation his high class rank won him assignment to the Army Corps of Engineers, which traditionally got the best and brightest West Point cadets.

Somervell distinguished himself in World War I, and established a reputation as one who could size up a problem, devise a solution, and drive a project through to a successful conclusion.

In the years between the wars Somervell headed up the New York Office of the Works Progress Administration (WPA), one of the nation's largest depression-era employers. The NY program was grossly inefficient and difficult to manage primarily because of the presence of powerful trade-unions and left wing influences. The WPA was administered by Harry Hopkins, FDR's alter-ego and close confidante.[4] Hopkins decided to call on the Army Corps of Engineers to bring some engineering expertise and some Army discipline to his agency, and he hired Somervell to take charge of the New York City office, which Hopkins considered his toughest job. In short order, Somervell transformed the NY WPA office into a smooth-running, profitable, multi-million dollar enterprise that efficiently built sewers, parks, playgrounds and roads.

Near the end of Somervell's tenure, the NY WPA built La Guardia Airport. La Guardia was made to order for Somervell. It was a $45 million project covering 558 acres. Somervell managed a workforce of 23,000 people, and to everyone's amazement, completed the project in just slightly over two years. The dedication of the airport in October, 1939 attracted 325,000 people, and in his dedication speech, Mayor Fiorello LaGuardia, for whom the airport was named, said that all the credit belonged to Somervell.[5]

Among those who attended the La Guardia Airport dedication was General George C. Marshall. *"I was quite impressed,"* Marshall wrote in a note he sent to Colonel Somervell, and he added Somervell's name to a short list he kept of officers who could be relied upon when the going got tough.

THE GAME PLAN COMES TOGETHER

When Secretary Stimson was introduced to Somervell at the Construction Division Office in early December, 1940, he felt he had a winner. After Somervell left, Stimson wrote in his diary, *"A gleam of light just came onto my horizon..."*

Stimson believed he had found his man, and he would not be disappointed. Somervell's first job was to house the fast-growing Army. Orders could not even be issued to the growing flood of new draftees and recruits because the Army had nowhere to send them. Somervell immediately put his entire staff on seven day work weeks, and he drove them until they were exhausted. He renamed his Construction Division "the shock troops of preparedness."[6]

By Spring, 1941, they had built fifty major camps, twenty-eight troop reception centers, nine hospitals, five munitions plants, fifty-two harbor facilities, and twenty-one storage depots. The War Department called it "the most remarkable achievement in rapid, large-scale construction in the annals of this or any other army."[7] Somervell's new facilities could now accommodate the entire Army, one million strong.

Sommervell's next job would be even more daunting – to create a new home for the War Department itself.

The War Department Before Somervell

At the beginning of 1941 the War Department had about 24,000 employees. They were spread around Washington DC, Virginia, and Maryland in 23 different buildings, including some apartment buildings and even a place called "Leary's Garage." Headquarters was the "Munitions Building," a converted factory that had been built as a temporary structure on the National Mall during World War I.[8]

Munitions Building in Washington DC

An obvious result of the space shortage was that senior officials often spent most of their days driving from one location to another rather than working. A major inconvenience in peacetime would become a disaster in war time.

A new War Department Building was already under construction and scheduled for completion in April, 1941, but unfortunately, it had been designed several years before when the Department was much smaller. The new building would have a total of 500,000 square feet, 270,000 of which would be suitable for offices. It was located in the Northwest Washington area called "Foggy Bottom."[9] Stimson calculated that it could reduce the total addresses from 23 to 17, but that it would still leave the Department one million square feet short of Washington DC office space. Further complicating an already dismal situation, the War Department was adding 1,000 new employees each month.

When the new Foggy Bottom building was ready for occupancy in April, Stimson refused to move his headquarters. He preferred to stay in the Munitions Building, and moved only the Army Corps of Engineers into Foggy Bottom.

Congress was aware of the problem and had already approved expenditures for more temporary buildings in Washington, but the War Department feared exacerbating already serious traffic and parking problems in the capital. Marshall appeared before the House Appropriations Committee in June to ask for permission to build temporary buildings in Arlington, Virginia. But unbeknownst to Stimson and Marshall, Somervell had a better idea. He believed that something bigger, better and more permanent was required.

A Bold and Audacious Plan

A Congressional Hearing had been scheduled for July 17, 1941, to discuss Marshall's request for temporary buildings in Arlington, Virginia to relieve the War Department's overcrowding. The hearing was called by powerful Virginia Democrat Clifton Woodrum, a Member of the House Appropriations Committee. Woodrum was considered a fiscal conservative, but like most lawmakers had a weakness for projects benefitting his home state. Brigadier General Eugene Reybold was the War Department's representative at the Hearing. Congressman Woodrum didn't like the idea of continued "band-aid" approach to the War Department's space problem, and after the Hearing he suggested that Reybold come up with a more permanent solution. Reybold asked for five days, and he immediately turned the project over to Somervell.[10] Woodrum's request was music to Somervell's ears. He immediately dispatched Major Pat Casey, one of the Army's brightest young engineers, to go over to Arlington and identify a site suitable for the building he had in mind, which would contain at least 4 million square feet of office space but would not be more than 3 stories high.[11] The building could not be a vertical high-rise for two reasons; first, a vertical building would require a steel frame and steel was on the government's list of restricted materials, and second, a vertical building would obstruct the lines of sight between Arlington Cemetery and the National Mall. The building Somervell envisioned would require a massive footprint, so acceptable sites would be few.

Casey felt that Somervell's preferred site, the old Washington-Hoover Airport, would not work due to horrible foundation problems. The site elevations were irregular, and most of the lower part was a swamp, subject to flooding. Casey picked a site called Arlington Farm, a half mile upriver from the airport, sitting just east of Arlington Cemetery. Somervell agreed to the site, and called in Edwin Bergstrom, the war Department's Chief Architect. Bergstrom was also president of the American Institute of Architects, the profession's most prestigious organization. It was Friday afternoon, and Somerville told Bergstrom and Casey he wanted plans for the building on his desk Monday morning.[12]

Brehon Burke Somervell

Somervell also assembled a group of 24 prominent consulting architects and engineers, most of whom were members of the American Society of Civil Engineers, the American Society of Mechanical Engineers, or the American Society of Landscape Architects. He anticipated running into Congressional resistance at some point during the process, and he wanted to be ready.

Bergstrom's team, Casey's team, and several of the consultants gathered at the Railroad Retirement Building in Washington on Friday afternoon and worked through the weekend to prepare the plans.

The Arlington Farm site covered about 70 acres and was kind of an irregular pentagon. The design team tried many layouts, including rectangles, octagons, and pentagons. The challenge was finding a way to squeeze the world's largest building, with 5 million square feet of floor space on three floors, inside the boundaries of the property.[13] The group refined the designs all through the weekend, and they finished on Sunday night. The building would be an asymmetrical pentagon, and it would have a total of 5.1 million square feet, of which 4 million would be office. Bergstom and Casey were in Somervell's office Monday morning with plans, renderings, and a construction estimate of $35 million. Bergstrom didn't know it at the time, but he had just designed the preliminary version of what would forever after be known as the Pentagon.

With plans in hand, Somervell immediately worked his way up the chain of command. He got approval from Deputy Chief of Staff General Moore, Chief of Staff General Marshall, and Deputy Secretary of War Robert Patterson. Next was Stimson, who was initially skeptical and somewhat embarrassed because a separate War Department Building was just being completed. However, Somervell's arguments gradually won Stimson over, and he finally gave his OK to sound the project out with Woodrum's Subcommittee.

Woodrum allowed Somervell to make the presentation to the Subcommittee, and they unanimously approved funding. Stimson decided it was now time to get the President on board, and Stimson brought it up at a Cabinet Meeting on July 24. Unbeknownst to Stimson, his timing with President Roosevelt could not have been better, and FDR quickly approved the project.

A Quick but Contentious Approval Process

Somervell was definitely on a roll! In one week he had proposed to build the world's largest building, had produced preliminary plans, had identified a satisfactory site, and had won preliminary approval from the War Department, the House Appropriations Subcommittee, and the President of the United States. Though he still needed approval from the full House and Senate, he must have believed that the hard part was behind him and anticipated clear sailing ahead. But Somervell would soon find out he was wrong, and that the project's stiffest resistance would come from where he least expected it.

The next obstacles for Somervell were the full House, the Senate Appropriations Committee, and the full Senate. The House passed the bill with only 11 dissenting votes, and passed it on the Senate. The Senate Appropriations Committee was no problem, because the project had the full support of powerful Committee Chairman Carter Glass of Virginia. But the full Senate was a different story. Few Senators opposed the project on its merits, but many were troubled both by building's size and the site. Those opposing the building's size worried about crippling, interminable traffic snarls that would surely ensue no matter where in the Washington area the building was located.

The camp opposing the site believed that it would desecrate the grand design layed out for the city by Pierre L'enfant in early the 1800s.[14] L'enfant's remains were interred in Arlington Cemetery on a hill overlooking the National Mall, which L'enfant had designed. They pointed out that the giant building at Arlington Farm would totally block the view from L'enfant's tomb. This camp had two aggressive spokesman; one was Gilmore D. Clarke, Chairman of the Commission on Fine Arts, and the other was Frederick Delano, Chairman of the National Capital Park & Planning Commission, who was also President Roosevelt's uncle ("Uncle Fred"). Both men lobbied hard to anyone who would listen for the Washington Hoover Airport south of the Cemetery. They referred to the project as "the rape of Washington."

Despite a lively and sometimes bitter debate in the full Senate on August 14, the Arlington Farm site and the full measure passed without amendment.

Thinking it was "game over," Somervell went to work preparing to break ground. He had already tapped John McShain, Inc. of Philadelphia as General Contractor, and on August 19 he brought Bergstrom, McShain, and his team together at Construction Division headquarters to go to work. Once again, however, Somervell had jumped the gun. Roosevelt had been out of Washington since August 9, and when he returned he had several urgent messages and strongly worded letters from both Clarke and Delano reminding him there were only a few days left to change the site and avoid what was in their view a huge mistake.

In 1917, as Assistant Secretary of the Navy, Roosevelt had persuaded President Wilson to allow temporary buildings to be erected on Constitution Avenue to alleviate the Army and Navy's severe space problems. Though his intent was that the buildings be demolished after the war, they were still there and represented an ugly blot on the Capital landscape. One of them was the Munitions Building, which now housed the senior staff of the War Department.[15] Roosevelt decided his legacy would be badly damaged if he repeated his mistake by once again desecrating the aesthetics of the capital, this time permanently.

On August 29, Roosevelt called Clarke and Somervell and asked them to come to the White House at 4:00. When they arrived FDR asked them to take a ride with him in the presidential limousine. They were all going to visit the two prospective sites and put an end to the debate. When they reached the Washington Hoover Airport site in Hell's Bottom, FDR stated that the site looked fine to him, and that he had decided it was where he wanted the building.[16]

THE RACE AGAINST TIME – CONSTRUCTION BEGINS

Somervell's winning streak at the War Department was over, but he was undaunted. Since the project was conceived he had promised he could complete the building in 12 months and begin relocating employees in six months. He might have to add a couple of months to the completion date to accommodate the foundation problems at the new site, but the target dates were his own, and had not been imposed on him by anyone else. A trait that made Somervell unique was that he never employed the conventional modus operandi of setting low expectations and then exceeding them. Instead, he set expectations impossibly high, and then figured out how to meet them. It is likely that no one on the project aside from Somervell himself really believed that people would be moving into the building on May 1, 1942.[17] But Somervell believed it, and that was what mattered.

Somervell had argued strenuously against the Hoover-Airport site because he understood the challenges that the poor soil conditions and irregular elevations would present to his engineers. But there was one advantage to the move. At the Arlington Farm site the shape of the building was dictated by the boundaries of the property. It had to be an irregular, asymmetrical pentagon to work. But at the new site this problem didn't exist, and a true pentagon could be used. General Contractor John McShain and his Superintendent Paul Hauck took advantage of the pentagon to develop a novel approach. The foundations and the superstructures for all five sides would be pretty much identical, so McShain would treat them as five separate buildings.[18] The start times would be staggered, but each building would have its own management, procurement staff, and construction crews. This "assembly-line" approach would stimulate competition among the teams and greatly reduce the potential mass confusion that might result from turning 15,000 workers loose on the entire building at one time.

On September 11, 1941 Somervell received word from Stimson that the revised contracts had all been signed, and that he was issuing the order to proceed. Somervell gathered his team and work began the same day on the E ring, furthest away from the Potomac. To compensate for the highly irregular elevations at the site, the building's foundation would have to rest upon footers and pilings, and McShain had eight pile drivers ready to go.[19]

Ear-splitting, Around-the-Clock Pounding

The first problem was what to use for pilings. The cheapest alternative was wood, but engineers feared that the moisture in the soil would limit the useful life of wood pilings. Steel would work fine, but steel was a restricted material and was thus in short supply. The answer, provided by a vendor, was "cast-in-place" concrete piles, which were corrugated sheet metal casings with a steel core fitted inside. The pile drivers pounded the steel mandrels into the ground until they met resistance, and then the mandrels were removed, leaving the empty steel casings, which were then filled with concrete. Each mandrel could be used over and over.

The pilings were driven in clusters of 3 to 12 each depending upon the load they would bear. Each piling could support a minimum weight of 30 tons. Each time a cluster was driven and filled, carpenters would build a four foot high wooden form around it and fill it with steel rebar. Then the form would be filled with concrete, forming a "pile cap." The pile caps together would form the "islands" on which the foundation would be laid.[20]

The pile driving began on the morning of September 12, 1941. Foundation drawings for only 20 pile caps were ready, so work began with only three of the eight pile drivers. Most piles had to be driven to twenty or thirty feet to hit bedrock, but that would increase to 50' to 60' as work moved closer to the river. More drawings were completed quickly, and soon the pounding became incessant and unrelenting. It went on round the clock. In two weeks 1,000 men were on the site and hundreds of piles had been sunk and capped. On September 25, the first part of the foundation slab was poured for Section A. Ultimately 41,492 piles would be driven, and, laid end to end they would cover more than 200 miles.[21] The 24-hour-a-day pounding would go for months.

Dredging, Excavating, Grading and Leveling

The Washington-Hoover site totaled 320 acres. Elevations varied from 8 feet to 55 feet above sea level. To raise the lower parts of the site above flood stage and to level the site sufficiently to accommodate roads and parking lots, it would be necessary to move 6 million cubic yards of earth, more earth than had ever been moved for any building in history. Popular Mechanics magazine, observing the project, predicted that the earth moving record would probably never be broken.

Potts & Callahan, the excavation and grading subcontractor, had never undertaken a project of anything close to this size, and in the project's first days they actually used some horse-drawn excavators to haul dirt.[22] By the time the job was completed, the Potts & Callahan fleet included 230 dump trucks, 60 tractors and bulldozers, 19 steam shovels, and 10 cranes (no horses).

The dump trucks caused all day traffic delays on heavily traveled Arlington Ridge Road, and half-mile backups became commonplace. The traffic problems and the hammering of the pile drivers both became constant irritants to residents of Arlington, Virginia.[23] Of course Somervell knew that neither of these activities would have been necessary on the Arlington Farm site, but he always looked forward instead of backward, and he never again brought the subject up.

The Tail Wags the Dog

One architect estimated that in normal circumstances, a year and a half would have been allowed to design a building of a this size. But Bergstrom's design team, then numbering over a hundred, had so far been given a total of 34 days to design the Pentagon.[24] Though the team was drafting furiously in a warehouse basement, they had produced only a small fraction of needed drawings. As a result, McShain was progressing at a snail's pace on the building. McShain had three thousand men on the job, but he wanted to have 3 or 4 times as many by this time. His men simply couldn't build anything unless Bergstrom provided timely drawings.

Superintendent Hauck began every day with a phone call to the designers asking what drawings they had ready for that day's work, and he was always disappointed by the answer. Finally, McShain decided to contact Colonel Leslie Groves, Somervell's Chief of Operations, to make him aware of the bottleneck. Groves assigned one of his top engineers, Paul Farrell, to investigate. Farrell's assessment was that there was no hope of the design team getting enough of a lead on the contractors to allow full speed ahead without additional reinforcements. Farrell reminded Groves that normally the design team would have had a several month head start over construction, and Bergstrom couldn't be blamed for that.

Somervell called William Delano, the architect on his LaGuardia Airport project, to ask him to suggest an architect who could organize the enormous effort that was needed to catch up. Delano without hesitation recommended Ides van Waterschoot van der Gracht, and van der Gracht was in Somervell's office the next day.[25] Somervell hired him on the spot and assigned him a small team of associates who would crisscross the United States recruiting the best talent they could find, paying them what the market required.[26]

The warehouse quickly became too small for the growing design team, and the team was moved into the vacated Eastern Airlines hangar at Washington Hoover.[27] The hangar had been built for airplanes, not draftsman, but it provided 16,000 square feet of unobstructed drafting space. In a short time Bergstrom and van der Gracht had grown the design team up to about 350 members. The team was running two Ozalid blueprint machines 24 hours a day, and they produced an average of 15,000 yards of blueprints each week.

To improve communications between the designers and the construction foremen, the architects also established a 100-

man field team of architects and engineers to advise and interpret drawings and make decisions on the site.[28] By the beginning of December 4,000 men were working at the site, 3,000 during the day and another 1,000 at night, driving piles and pouring concrete. The nighttime work was lighted by brilliant flares.[29] Although the team was finally developing some speed, a November 15 audit showed that the project was only 2% complete.

Realizing that at the present pace the work would take eight years to complete, Somervell pulled out all stops. To that point engineers had tightly regulated the pouring of concrete to prevent unsightly shrinkage cracking. Somervell ordered his team to begin pouring slabs as big and fast as possible, "cracks be damned." Speed of construction took precedence over all other considerations from that point forward.[30]

Attack on Pearl Harbor Turns up the Heat

On Sunday, December 7, the Japanese attacked Pearl Harbor. The attack not only changed the world, but it would have a profound impact on progress at the Pentagon. The attack's most immediate result was to end all discussions about making the building smaller. It was suddenly apparent even to its critics that the building needed to provide the maximum possible office space. Sommervell had never really planned to reduce the building's size anyway, but now he no longer needed to be coy about it. He could build an even larger headquarters than he himself had ever planned. Congressmen and commissions who had been apoplectic about the building's cost and who fought every new appropriation request to the death were suddenly in full retreat as patriotism overwhelmed budgetary considerations. In the words of one of his officers "We now had a blank check."[31]

Somervell, over the loud protests of his architects and contractors, announced that he was moving up the already impossible schedule. He would now have 1 million square feet ready for occupancy by April 1 instead of May 1.[32]

However, the war hysteria had also aroused new concerns in the War Department which nearly stopped progress dead in its tracks and threatened to blow up the entire schedule. The Chain of Command wondered whether security had been given sufficient attention during the planning stage. Within days of the attack the Department approved $3 million to excavate 300,000 square feet of additional basement for a bomb shelter, and some officers remembered that FDR had originally wanted a building without windows. Many now believed that the issue of windows had to be revisited and that the entire building should now be bomb-proofed.[33] After about a week of sometimes heated meetings, Somervell prevailed and the certainty of a long delay triumphed over the possibility of bombs and broken windows. By mid-January 6,000 men were on the job and things were finally moving. By January 21, plans and specifications were no longer delaying work, and the design team had caught up.

Overhead View of Worksite – January 17, 1942

The Final Push

Based upon the recent attack by the Japanese and the attendant changes to the size of the building, Somervell made one more update of his promised completion dates. He would now be moving the first employees in on May 1, which had been his first projection back in September, and the building would be completed on November 15, 1942. That gave him about 3½ months to have 1 million square feet ready.[34]

After having completed much of one section of the building, the workers were finally finding a rhythm. The concrete pours were now continuous, 24 hours a day. On the bank of the nearby Potomac lagoon, the concrete plant was producing about 7,000 tons of concrete daily, which required 5,500 tons of sand and gravel, 900 tons of concrete, and 115,000 gallons of water.[35]

Fortunately, the Potomac itself provided a pretty much inexhaustible supply of sand, gravel, and water. Engineers calculated that more than ½ of the building's total weight came from the Potomac River.[36] By way of comparison, the Pentagon would require 410,000 cubic yards of concrete, almost 7 times more than the Empires State Building.

The constant pouring of concrete meant that the carpenters had to race to keep up with their constant supply of forms. The carpenters used an assembly line process to build forms for the columns, beams, slabs, and walls. The total job required more than twenty-three million board feet of lumber.[37] In late March the building was 40% complete and 13,000 workers were on the job. It would soon increase to 15,000.

On April 22, Somervell's deputy Brigadier General "Fat" Steyer issued the orders. Employees of the Ordnance Department would begin moving into the Pentagon at 8:00am on April 30.[38] The new employees were not going to like their new venue. There would be no heat or air conditioning, it was not certain that the cafeteria would be ready, the plaster would not be thoroughly dry, and there would still be leaks and other "problems" for awhile, but Somervell would not relent. He reiterated he wanted them in the building and at their desks working on May 1, regardless of discomfort.[39]

On July 21st the decision was made to add an entire fifth floor to the Pentagon, and the completion date was extended by two months, from November 15 to January 15, 1943.[40]

The site in July, 1942, after the First Workers had Moved In

THE PENTAGON BY THE NUMBERS

The Pentagon was completed on schedule, 483 days after groundbreaking.[41] The first employees moved into the building only 230 days after groundbreaking. The building contains 6.636 million square feet of floor space, and its footprint covers 34 acres. The entire site takes up 583 acres, and includes 200 acres of lawn and 67 acres of parking which will accommodate 8,770 cars. There are 30 miles of access roads with 21 bridges and overpasses, and the building houses a shopping concourse, snack bars, cafeterias, dining rooms, banks, a subway station, and a bus platform.[42]

During its peak usage in WWII, 33,000 employees worked at the Pentagon.[43]

The building rests upon 41,492 reinforced concrete pilings.

Five and ½ million cubic feet of earth had to be moved during construction and 900,000 tons of concrete were poured. The Pentagon has 17.5 miles of corridors and 7,734 windows.[44] Despite the maze of corridors, it takes only 7 minutes to walk between any two points in the building. The 5 acre, pentagonal Central Courtyard has always been referred to as "Ground Zero," as it would very likely be the first target for any country attacking the United States. The Pentagon has its own zip code.

LASTING CULTURAL HERITAGE

The opening of the Pentagon for business on May 1 was an extraordinary achievement, and the Washington Post called it "a remarkable feat." Its most outstanding feature is the speed with which it was built. The Pentagon was occupied by employees less than 8 months after it was conceived, and it was completed in sixteen months. The Pentagon has become the ultimate symbol of American power and independence, and for more than seventy years it has inspired Americans to work harder and build better.

The Pentagon today

The driving force behind the construction of the Pentagon was Brigadier General Brehon Burke Somervell. Somervell was driven by what one officer described as *"an abiding sense of urgency."*[45] He actually stopped signing his middle initial to save time during the war.[46] During his Army career Somervell declared all-out war against bureaucracy, and he fired more than a dozen generals, and whole squads of colonels.

Somervell was promoted from Lieutenant Colonel to 3-star General in less than one year.[47] On February 28, 1942, about half way into the building of the Pentagon, President Roosevelt issued an Executive Order dividing the Army into three commands, and made Somervell Commander of All Army Supply forces. The New York Times described Somervell's new job this way: *"Not even Napoleon's Quartermaster could approach the magnitude of the job Somervell had to do – supplying 8 million troops scattered all over the world."*[48] In their official account of World War II, describing the world-wide mobilization of supplies, Fine and Remington wrote: *"In urgency, complexity, and difficulty, the undertaking surpassed anything the world had ever seen."* And in December of 1945, announcing Somervell's retirement, Secretary of War Robert W. Patterson said: *"In organizing and directing the worldwide supply lines upon which our troops depended for their offensive power, General Somervell performed a service without parallel in the annals of military history."*[49]

Somervell died from a heart attack at this home in Ocala, Florida on February 13, 1955. The Washington Post lauded Somervell as *"one of the ablest officers the United States Army has ever produced."*[50]

CHAPTER 5

THE SS UNITED STATES

Since her maiden voyage on July 3, 1952, the *SS United States* has been almost universally acclaimed as the greatest ocean liner ever built. Like all great man-made icons, the *"Big U,"* as she was called, required the collaboration of many people and many institutions. But more than any other of this country's epic engineering achievements, the *Big U* resulted from the work of one man, and that man was William Francis Gibbs.

THE GOLDEN AGE OF OCEAN TRAVEL

The glorious days of passenger ocean liners began around 1830, with the first scheduled crossings by the "packet ships," and continued until the early 1960s when the advent of jet airliners finally ended their reign. The first passenger ships were the Clippers, giant sailing ships powered by wind, which required an average of 40 days to make a westward crossing.[1] The Clippers evolved into steam-driven, side paddle wheelers, which eventually gave way to propeller-driven vessels powered by giant steam turbines, the fastest of which could make the crossing in either direction in between four and five days.

During the first half of the twentieth century the Ocean Liner represented the epitome of glamorous travel. An ocean crossing was a great adventure, and each ship was an exciting showplace, replete with beautifully decorated cabins, outstanding meals and superlative service. Frequent travelers knew the names of all the best ships and their crossing schedules. The biggest ships each carried more than 2,000 passengers, and the passenger manifests almost always included the names of an interesting mix of diplomats, actors, entertainers, and business moguls. Cunard was the most famous of all the great passenger lines, and for many years its primary advertising pitch was *"Getting There is Half the Fun!"*[2]

The Blue Riband

The Blue Riband is an award given to the passenger liner making the westward crossing of the Atlantic in regular service at the highest average speed.[3] Average speed is used instead of shortest time because the ships follow different routes. The award is based upon the Westward crossing because of the increased difficulty resulting from sailing against the Gulf Stream currents. The traditional route for the Blue Riband liners ran 3,000 miles from Bishop's Rock by Cornwall, England to the Ambrose Lighthouse at the entrance to New York harbor.[4] The Blue Riband is not well known to the public, but has been highly coveted by all the passenger lines and their flag countries since 1830.

The Blue Riband trophy

During the 130 years from 1830 to 1960 a total of 35 transatlantic liners held the Blue Riband, beginning with *Columbia* in 1830 and ending with *SS United States* which still holds the trophy. A "Blue Riband Crossing," like the trophy itself, was a

Westward crossing from Bishop's Rock to Ambrose Light which broke the existing record for highest average speed. Of the thousands of crossings that were made over 130 years, only 60 were Blue Riband Crossings.

Supremacy on the Atlantic

Of the 35 passenger liners that held the Blue Riband prior to 1950, twenty-five carried the British flag, five the German flag, three the American flag, and one each the French and Italian flags.[5] Thirteen of the British flag ships which had held Blue Riband were owned by the fabled Cunard Line. From the 1860s to 1950 every holder of the Blue Riband flew a European flag, and when the *SS United States* was launched in 1952, no US flag ship had owned the Blue Riband since 1854.[6] Clearly, supremacy on the Atlantic belonged to Great Britain and the Europeans, and the United States was barely a factor.

The first half of the twentieth century was the era of the great "ships of state," and the United States never mounted a serious challenge for the Blue Riband. But in 1916 Walter Francis Gibbs, then 29, and his brother Frederick, then 27, almost changed that. They procured a commitment from International Mercantile Marine, owned by JP Morgan, Jr., to build two $30 million super liners.[7] Morgan was recovering from the Titanic disaster and the recent death of his Father, and he became convinced that the Gibbs brothers' proposal could help IMM finally establish American supremacy at sea. Unfortunately, the US Declaration of War against Germany on April 6, 1917 ended Morgan's hopes and a potentially great project for the Gibbs brothers.

Undaunted, William Francis Gibbs would raise the issue of national pride often and effectively during his continuing quest to build the world's greatest ocean liner.

The Merchant Marine

To fully appreciate the difficulties faced by Gibbs and other Naval architects as they designed the great ships of the day it is helpful to understand the concept of the merchant marine.

Stated simply, a merchant marine is a fleet of ships that carries paying passengers and commercial cargo during peace time, and military troops and war materials in wartime.[8] Most countries have a merchant marine, but the statutes governing the ownership and operation of the ships vary significantly among countries. The US merchant marine was established by the Jones Act of 1920 and now operates under the Merchant Marine act of 1936, which established the US Maritime Commission and also authorized government subsidies for the construction and operation of merchant vessels.[9]

Although the availability of subsidies was welcomed by fleet operators, the Merchant Marine Act complicated the jobs of naval architects and shipbuilders. In essence, large ships had to be designed and built for two separate owners. Commercial profitability depended upon luxury, beautifully outfitted common areas, and hospitality, but the Navy focused on quick refitting, steed bed dormitories, fireproofing, troop movement capability, combat survivability and dimensions that enabled passage through the Panama Canal. To procure financing and maximize subsidies, it was now necessary for a ship to satisfy the conflicting requirements of both commercial banks and the US Navy. In essence, every ship really had to be two ships in one, but owners and lenders expected two ships for the price of one.

WILLIAM FRANCIS GIBBS

William Francis Gibbs was born in Philadelphia in 1886 to William Warren and Frances Ayres Gibbs, and William's brother Frederic was born two years later. William Warren

Gibbs was a financial speculator whose fortunes rose and fell frequently.[10] In 1886 his fortunes were rising and he was regarded as one of Philadelphia's wealthiest men.

Formative Events

In November, 1894, Gibbs took his sons William and Frederic, then eight and six years old, to the Cramp Shipyard in Philadelphia to witness the launch of the *St. Louis*, at the time the world's third largest passenger ship.[11] It was William Francis' first up-close look at a great ship, and he and Frederic shared the ceremony with 25,000 others, including President and Mrs. Grover Cleveland. The great ship displayed flags of many nations topped off by the American flag waving high above the ship's bow. Throughout the remainder of his life William Francis Gibbs never forgot that experience and recalled it as the day he dedicated his life to ships.

Certainly, from that day in 1894 forward, young Gibbs thought about little else but ships. He graduated from Delancy School in Philadelphia in 1905, and at his father's wish he entered Harvard the next year. But from almost his first day in Cambridge Gibbs was preoccupied with ships. He knew that at that very time the Cunard Line was building the two greatest ships in the world, the *Lusitania* and the *Mauretania.* Not only would they be the largest ships afloat, but they would be the first to use steam turbines and also the first to feature 4 propellers instead of 2.[12] William Francis was determined to sail on both ships.

Although his financial fortunes were in decline at the time, William Warren Gibbs was somehow persuaded by his two sons to book them round trip passages to Europe. They would go over on the *Lusitania* on October 1, 1907, and return on the *Mauretania* on November 16.[13] Prior to sailing William Francis had read everything written about the two ships, but he had to see things for himself. While other passengers were enjoying their staterooms and the beautiful salons, William and Frederic were all over the ships, observing and taking notes. The Gibbs Brothers had chosen the right ships for their research. The *Lusitania* won the Blue Riband on only her second voyage, and *Mauretania* would hold the coveted trophy for twenty years, from 1909 to 1929.[14]

Rendering of The Mauretania – Circa 1907

The Financial Panic of 1907 and Law School

Upon disembarking from the Mauretania in New York the brothers learned that the Panic of 1907 (aka "The Banker's Panic") had seriously impacted their father's finances.[15] Taking place over a three week period beginning in mid-October and ending in early November, the financial panic destroyed many personal fortunes, apparently including that of the senior Mr. Gibbs.

William Francis soon re-entered Harvard, but lived a much more Spartan life than he had previously. He dropped out of Harvard in 1910 without a degree, and enrolled at Columbia. He graduated from Columbia University in 1913 with degrees in Law and Economics.[16] Gibbs hated both the study and the practice of law, but to fulfill a promise to his father, he went to work for a New York City law firm after graduation, and provided money to his cash-strapped family regularly. William Francis faithfully returned home to Philadelphia every weekend so that he and Frederic could continue work on their drawings and blueprints.

It was soon 1915, and, though William still practiced law, he was devoting more and more time to his ships.

IMM, JP Morgan, and a Near Miss at The Dream

After about a year of working weekends in their cramped quarters in Philadelphia, the Gibbs brothers had roughed out a prototype of the their dream ship, and preliminary drawings were ready for presentation. Their ship would be 1,001 feet long and would have a propulsion system that would make it much faster than *Mauretania,* the world's fastest ship at the time. William Francis believed he had designed out all of the flaws in the best existing vessels as he developed his prototype.

The Gibbs brothers were realists, and they knew the odds were stacked against them. Neither brother had any formal training in ship design nor any list of past successes. They also knew that the universe of companies with both the motive and the ability to make such a huge financial commitment was very small. In fact, William believed there was only one viable candidate, International Mercantile Marine ("IMM"). IMM was owned by John Pierpont Morgan, Jr. ("Jack"), the son of famous banking magnate JP Morgan, who had financed the *Titanic.* The senior Morgan had died in 1913 and left his son a $69 million bequest.[17] William knew that to have any chance of a face to face meeting with Jack Morgan he would first have to secure active support for project from the best and most respected people in the ship building business. He immediately went to work on selling his design to three people; a respected engine manufacturer, the world's foremost hull designer, and the CEO of a great railroad.

To move his ship at speeds above 30 knots William would need engines that could generate at least 180,000 horsepower, and no such engines had ever been built. He knew that William Leroy Emmet, the Chief Engineer at General Electric, had developed a new engine system known as the "GE-Curtis Turbo Generator" that was being used in the newest US electric power plants, and he believed the system was adaptable to large passenger ships.[18] Gibbs also knew that Emmet was looking for new markets.

William Gibbs had an old college friend who arranged a meeting with Emmet for him, and in late 1915 the brothers walked into Emmet's office with their plans and drawings. William convinced Emmet that, using the Turbo Generator, his ocean liner could increase the top speed of *Mauretania* by 20%. Before the meeting ended William secured Emmet's commitment that GE would design the engines for his ships, and the Gibbs brothers used that commitment to help open their next door, that with Rear Admiral David W. Taylor, the world's foremost hull designer and Chief of Construction for the US Navy.[19] Early in his Naval career, Taylor had been selected to study marine engineering at the Royal Naval College in Greenwich, England, and had posted the highest grades ever achieved by any student up to that time.

Taylor made some minor tweaks to William's design and then offered to build a 40 foot long scale model of his ship for testing at the US Navy Experimental Model Basin. One month later William walked into the test basin, where a 41.7 foot scale model labeled *"Proposed American Passenger Steamship"* was waiting. When the model was tested in the model basin at the equivalent of 180,000 horsepower, it moved smoothly through the water at the equivalent of 33 knots, exactly 27% faster than *Mauretania*.[20]

William and Frederic had one more stop, and that was at the offices of Ralph Peters, President of the *Long Island Railroad.*

They knew that if a shipping terminal could be built outside of New York City at Montauk Point, a percentage of the railroad freight moving to and from New York could be diverted to Montauk Point via *Long Island Railroad* . When Peters saw the plans for the Montauk terminal and the passenger liner's design his interest was piqued, and when he was shown the stamps of approval from GE and Admiral Taylor he was hooked. He immediately called Jack Morgan and set up a meeting.[21]

At the meeting with IMM William presented the plans for his project, which included the two largest and fastest passenger ships ever built and a shipping terminal at Montauk Point. The total estimated cost was $75 million, which was 7 X more than JP Morgan had invested in *Titanic* a few years earlier. Jack Morgan agreed that he would finance the project and that IMM would pay William and Frederic salaries to prepare the final plans, designs, drawings and documentation.

William believed his dream had become reality, and he immediately resigned his position at the New York law firm. He could not have known that World War I was about to put his dream on hold.

A German Giant is Reincarnated in America

When the First World War broke out on July, 28, 1914, *Vaterland,* the world's largest passenger liner, was docked at the Hoboken Pier in New York City.[22] German headquarters decided that their prize ship was safer in a neutral port than on the open seas, and they ordered her to stay in New York. Almost three years later when the United States declared war on Germany, she was still in Hoboken, and 200 American soldiers stormed the ship and seized it as a "prize of war." President Wilson renamed it *"Leviathan."*[23] During the remainder of the War the former German flagship would transport almost 120,000 American soldiers to the war front, as many as

14,000 per voyage.

When the *Leviathan* was decommissioned after the war the Wilson Shipping Board wanted her returned to passenger service under the US flag. The giant ship had been gutted during her wartime service, and she need a complete restoration, renovation and refitting. In November of 1919 the Shipping board assigned *Leviathan* to IMM for "management and operation," and IMM asked the Gibbs Brothers, still employed at IMM, to prepare a plan for the restoration. A new design with detailed drawings was to be completed by November, 1921. When it was leaked to the press that the Shipping Board planned to actually convey *Leviathan's* ownership to IMM a major political firestorm blew up. Powerful newspaper icon William Randolph Hearst accused the Wilson Administration of collusion with IMM and the Morgan interests, and the ownership transfer never happened.[24]

Warren G. Harding became President in March of 1921, and he appointed Albert Lasker Chairman of the Shipping Board. Lasker was impressed by the work of the Gibbs Brothers, but wanted to cut all ties with IMM over the scandal.[25] He asked Gibbs to complete the *Leviathan* redesign under contract directly to the Shipping Board that bypassed IMM. William and Frederic left IMM, established Gibbs Brothers, Inc., and completed the restoration plans on schedule at the end of November. Lasker then asked Gibbs to oversee and manage the restoration project for a fee of $182,000.

Newport News Shipbuilders submitted the low bid of $5,595,000 and the work began. *Leviathan* completed her sea trials on July 19, 1923, and began regular passenger service as the flagship of newly formed United States Lines. The five years that William had devoted to *Leviathan* had pulled he and Frederic away from their own superliner project, but the high profile *Leviathan* had enhanced their bona fides in the industry which would serve them well going forward. William

Francis Gibbs was only thirty-seven years old, and the dream still burned brightly.

The Years Between the Wars

The Roaring twenties didn't roar for the US passenger ship business. Prohibition made it very difficult for American flag ships to compete against the Europeans, whose ships still had open bars.[26] The *Leviathan* was losing money and there was little interest in building another superliner. The twenties were lean years for Gibbs & Co. Inc., as well, but the Company managed to win enough design commissions to stay afloat.

The Matson Lines MALOLO in 1926 – A Gibbs Design

The Gibbs team designed four medium-sized passenger liners for the Matson Lines, including the *Malolo*, which greatly enhanced Gibbs & Co.'s reputation for always putting safety first. During its sea trials *Malolo* was rammed midships by the Norwegian freighter *Jacob Christiansen*.[27] The *Malolo* did not capsize nor did she sink, and there were no injuries. Gibbs also designed four somewhat smaller liners for the Grace Lines, which sailed to the Carribean Islands and the West Coast via the Panama Canal. The Grace ships were known as the "Santas," and included the *Santa Rosa, Santa Paula, Santa Lucia,* and *Santa Elena.*[28]

All eight of these ships would serve as US troop carriers during the War.

In 1929, to broaden the Company's revenue base, William and Frederic brought in Daniel Cox as a full partner. Cox was a renowned yacht builder, and William believed he would bring in additional revenues.[29] That plan did not work, and William bought Cox out in 1932, leaving the Company's name unchanged.

Franklin Delano Roosevelt was elected President in 1932, and almost immediately began to rebuild the American Navy. Roosevelt and Willam Francis Gibbs knew each other and shared common interests and experiences. Both attended Harvard and both held degrees from Columbia Law School. Both were experts on naval architecture and maritime history. FDR was an avid sailor and passionate model ship builder.[30] Their friendship remained off the record, but Gibbs employees later recalled numerous telephone conversations between the two. Beginning in the late 1930s and continuing to War's end, Gibbs & Co., designed thousands of American war ships and cargo carriers, including destroyers, landing craft, minesweepers, tankers, cruisers, and Liberty ships. Between 1940 and 1945 Gibbs & Cox designed 74% of all America naval vessels, and at the height of the war the Company had over 1,000 employees.[31]

In 1938 Gibbs and Cox won a commission to design a passenger liner for the United States Lines. The ship would be 725 feet long, 95 feet wide, and would carry 1,438 passengers in three classes. The ship would be christened *SS America*, and would make her maiden voyage in 1940.[32]

SS America in 1940 – Clearly Marked as Neutral in Wartime

WAR'S END – MAKING THE DREAM A REALITY

The United States emerged from the war stronger than it had ever been, without any serious economic competitors. William Francis Gibbs had established himself as the country's foremost naval architect, and Gibbs & Cox employed a team of engineers and designers that was arguably the best in the world.[33] Cunard still ruled the seas, then with the Queen Mary (holder of the Blue Riband) and the Queen Elizabeth, but Gibbs believed that all the pieces were finally in place for him to realize his childhood dream of building the world's fastest and greatest ship. He was 59 years old, and he knew it was time to go for the proverbial brass ring.

The Merchant Marine Act of 1936 had replaced the Shipping Board with the Maritime Commission, and an ailing President Roosevelt had directed the Commission to rebuild the merchant marine with a new fleet of comfortable passenger liners. Though Roosevelt died in April of 1945, President Truman vowed to follow through on rebuilding the fleet. The United States Lines owned the country's premier passenger fleet. Its President was Brigadier General John Franklin, and its largest stockholder was Vincent Astor, who had committed his formidable financial strength to the business.[34] Gibbs decided that a meeting with John Franklin at United States Lines was the place to start, and he and his team began the process of refining their superliner prototype in preparation for the big meeting. They labeled the updated the new superliner prototype "Design 12201."[35]

The Design 12201 Prototype

Gibbs would pitch Design 12201 to Franklin as the finest, fastest, safest, and most beautiful ship ever built. The crucial design elements would be a "low prismatic coefficient" (slim hull below the waterline), a low center of gravity, a shallow draft, a very high power to weight ratio, and what Gibbs referred to as "the power of survival." The design team would be led by Walter Bachman, who Gibbs referred to as "the greatest marine engineer in the world."[36] In less than a week the Gibbs & Cox designers and engineers brought William the results of their work.

The ship would be a low, sleek superliner with a length of 990 feet and a beam (width) of 101 feet. It would have an extremely low prismatic coefficient of .559, and an all-aluminum superstructure which would greatly reduced her weight and lower her center of gravity. Design 12201 had a draft (distance from the waterline to the keel) of only 31 feet, and she displaced only 45,000 tons of water.[37] By contrast *Queen Mary*, only slightly longer and wider, had a draft of 40 feet and displaced 80,000 tons of water. From the safety standpoint, Design 12201 would be a "five compartment" ship, meaning that with up to five of its twenty watertight compartments flooded the ship would remain afloat, and it would also have two separate engine rooms, so that if one were hit by a torpedo the ship could continue to sail.[38]

The ship would have four steam turbines which could generate a maximum of 240,000 shaft horsepower.[39] The ship would have a sustained service speed of 34 knots (almost 40 mph), which was unprecedented for a passenger ship. Gibb's brother Frederic estimated the ship would cost $50 million to build.

Selling the Super Liner

In early 1946 the Gibbs brothers had two meetings with Brigadier General Franklin of US Lines. On February 4, they let him know that they had designs for two new passenger liners, designs 11811 and 12201. They explained that 11811 was a streamlined vessel that incorporated their most advanced technologies, but that it would not challenge the *Queens* for supremacy, because it would be only about 850 feet long. Design 12201, on the other hand, would be the fastest, safest, and most beautiful ship afloat, and would make United States Lines the preeminent player in world shipping. Knowing that Franklin planned to seek the largest possible subsidy from the new US Maritime Commission, Gibbs let him know that either design could be converted into the world's fastest troop carrier in 48 hours.[40]

In their second meeting a month later, Franklin informed the brothers that he wanted to move ahead with Design 12201 if the ship could deliver a sustainable service speed of 33 knots and be built for $50 million. William committed Gibbs & Cox to those targets, and Franklin was sold. On March 26, 1946, he sent a letter to the US Maritime Commission informing the members that, with a 50% subsidy from the Commission, US Lines planned to build a new transatlantic passenger liner that would incorporate all the wartime advances in shipbuilding technology, that would be fireproof, that could be quickly be converted into a troop carrier, and that could pass through the Panama Canal.[41] Franklin told Commission members he was confident his new ship would ensure American dominance of the North Atlantic sea lanes for the next twenty years.

Gibbs with His Ever-present Hat

A full year passed before President Truman formed a five-person advisory committee to prepare recommendations on rebuilding the merchant marine, and another eight months passed before the committee submitted its report. By then it was November of 1947. The US Lines Board of Directors had approved the purchase of the new ship represented by Design 12201, but had capped its maximum investment at $25 million.[42]

Frederic Gibbs, the numbers man for Gibbs & Cox, was becoming concerned that as time passed rapidly escalating post-war labor and materials costs were going to increase his original $50 million estimate for Design 12201.[43] Since the US Line's investment was fixed, any increase would require the Maritime Commission's construction subsidy to exceed its mandated 50% limit. The Commission's mandate allowed it to exceed the 50% guideline only for "compelling" national security reasons.[44]

Frederic's concerns were well-founded. The low bid to build the ship came in at $67,350,000, and with fixtures, equipment and fees it became $71 million. Knowing this number could be a deal breaker, William and Frederic had to come up with a new approach. They asked the Newport News yard to bid the job as a "normal" ship, without any of the national defense features. That bid came back at about $45 million. Prior to reporting the higher number to the Maritime Commission, William called another meeting with the US Lines executive team.

They decided to ask the Commission to subsidize 45% of the cost of the "normal and unusual" ship, which would be about $20 million, but to ask it to pay for all the national defense features, the rationale being that these features added nothing to the profitability of operating the liner.[45] So in total, US Lines would contribute $25 million, and the Commission $45 million.

On April 7, 1949, the four members of the Maritime Commission, Brigadier General Franklin, and William Francis Gibbs began what would be a three-day marathon meeting to resolve the impasse. Finally, at the end of day three, Commissioner Mellon offered to break the 2 to 2 vote among the commissioners and support the project.[46]

The contract for construction of the super liner was signed on May 8, 1949, and it was agreed that the name of the ship would be the *SS United States*.[47] The signing took place 33 years after work had begun work on the project, and Gibbs was now 63 years old. He believed his dream ship was now safe from politicians, but he would be proven wrong.

Building the Dream Ship

On February 8, 1950, the first keel plate was laid for SS United States at the Newport News shipyard.[48] William Francis Gibbs was there long with a group of shipyard executives, naval Officers, and reporters. But this would be the last day for the

The hull of SS United States. The 5-blade inboard propeller was a Gibbs & Cox innovation that eliminated cavitation, the shaking that all large ocean liners of the day experienced at sea speeds.

reporters. Shortly after construction began, Gibbs banned all reporters, photographers and cameras from the site.[49] He ordered that all plans and drawings be kept under lock and key, and all 3,000 workers at the site were instructed not to talk to anyone about the ship. Although Gibbs technically had no ownership in the ship, he was on the site every day, watching over everything. All 3,000 workers knew who he was, and knew he was watching.

President Truman had never been happy that his US Maritime Commission had agreed to subsidize 65% of the ship's construction cost, and, a few months after construction began, he abolished the Commission and replaced it with a new agency, the Federal Maritime Board and Maritime Administration.[50] In September, Gibbs received a frantic call from one of the ship's contractors. He was told that US Lines had instructed them to cease all work on the ship, as the *SS United States* was being seized by the Pentagon for conversion to a troop ship.[51] The outbreak of the Korean War had caught the country off guard, and the Pentagon needed ships.

Everyone associated with the project was devastated by the news, except for William Francis Gibbs, who seemed unfazed.

He had suspected that Secretary of Defense Louis Johnson was preparing to make this move, and he quietly asked his staff to continue working on the project, promising the decision would be reversed. On September 19, a few days after Johnson's decision, he was called into the Oval Office by President Truman and fired. Johnson was quickly replaced by retired General George C. Marshall, author of the Marshall Plan and former Secretary of State. On November 1, 45 days after the seizure, Marshall announced that he had reversed Johnson's decision, and that *SS United States* would be completed as a commercial passenger liner.[52] It is not known what happened during that 45-day period, but no one was asking.

The great ship was nearing completion in the Spring of 1951, and a launch date was scheduled for June 23, 1951. By 5:00 on the morning of June 23, SS United States was fully afloat and ready. Not including the 45 during which she was "seized" by Secretary Johnson, she had been built in 455 days.[53] The launch had created the biggest traffic jam in the history of Newport News. Several speakers took the speaker's podium in the hot afternoon sun. Brigadier John Franklin, President of United States Lines, noted in his remarks:

> *"The SS United States is essentially the same ship that my Father, Philip Franklin, hoped to build back in 1916, when he met with JP Morgan, Jr. and two young men from Philadelphia, William and Frederic Gibbs."*[54]

William Francis Gibb's wife Vera joined him for the historic day. She wrote in her diary *"He was attired in his khaki overalls, and I had never seen him look happier."*

SS United States would stand at her outfitting pier for 10 months while her interior decorators did their work, but on May 14, 1952, as the sun rose in Newport News, the ship's great engines came to life and she headed out to the open sea for her speed trials. The ship was packed with 1,669 passengers and a full crew, but this was not a luxury cruise. It was to see whether the great ship, fully loaded, could really achieve the speeds for which she had been designed. Gibbs, as was his custom at sea trials, would spend the entire voyage watching the gauges and making sure no unauthorized person got a peek.[55] No one would know how fast the ship really went until 1977, after she had been retired and the Navy declassified her design features.

SS United States in New York Harbor with familiar landmarks

ACCOMPLISHMENTS WHILE IN SERVICE

On her maiden voyage which left New York on June 3, 1952, *SS United States* broke the Eastward speed record held by *Queen Mary* by more than 10 hours, averaging 35.59 knots.[57] As she arrived in Southampton, she received a cable from British Prime Minister Winston Churchill saying "Congratulations on your wonderful achievement." On her return she took the coveted Blue Riband by breaking Westward record by more than 9 hours.[58]

The "Big U" had the greatest power to weight ratio ever achieved in a commercial passenger liner, and she was capable of steaming non-stop for over 12,000 miles at a cruising speed of 35 knots. She was the largest passenger liner ever built in the United States, the first to be built entirely in drydock, and the first to be fully air-conditioned. She could carry 1,972 passengers in 693 staterooms, along with 900 crew members . Big U was equipped with 24 double-hulled aluminum lifeboats, each with motive power and a capacity of 140 passengers.[59]

During her 17-year service career *SS United States* made 400 round trip, transatlantic voyages at 30 knots plus and had an exemplary safety record. She was universally acclaimed as the fastest, safest, most beautiful ship afloat.

Leaving New York Harbor for Southampton on one of 400 voyages

LASTING CULTURAL LEGACY

The great ship *SS United States* was retired by United States Lines in December, 1969 after a glorious 17-year service career that spanned 400 voyages. It had simply become impossible for the passenger lines to profitably compete against jet air travel. In the years following the Great War William Francis Gibbs had proven that a great man in a great country could still do what most people thought impossible. He was able to once again demonstrate American exceptionalism by reestablishing her supremacy at sea for the first time in 100 years.

> *"This great ship," Gibbs said, "is the embodiment to me of the force and power of a free people working with individual initiative, coming together and cooperating to produce a result far beyond the capacity of any individual to produce by himself..."*[60]

At the declassification meeting in 1977 naval architects and engineers from all over the world would only have one question: What was the top speed of *SS United States?* The answer was an astonishing 38.32 knots per hour, convertible to almost 45 land miles per hour, a speed which was never approached by any other ocean liner.[56]

William Francis Gibbs died on September 6, 1967 at the age of 81.[61] General Franklin of US Lines died in 1975 at age 79, and Frederic Gibbs passed in 1980 at the age of 90.

Gibbs & Cox, Inc. is still doing business and still lists the US Navy as one of its clients.

The *SS United States* rests at Pier 84 in South Philadelphia, a short distance from the old Cramp Shipyard where Gibbs watched the christening of *St. Louis* in 1904.[62] She is now owned by the SS United States Conservancy, which is "dedicated to the preservation and restoration of the SS United States." The Executive Director of the SS United States Conservancy is Susan Gibbs, the granddaughter of William Francis Gibbs.[63]

CHAPTER 6

1953 TO 2015
A LOSS OF DOMINANCE

Much is written today about the decline of America. If measured by remarkable architectural and engineering achievements, the decline is very real indeed. Since completion of the Pentagon in 1953, the United States has clearly lost its position of supremacy as a developer of great mega-projects. Evidence of decline is everywhere, and here are examples.

HIGH DAMS

At its completion in 1935, Hoover Dam represented a breakthrough in dam engineering and a great example of American ingenuity. It remains so today. Many of the advances made at Hoover became standard dam building protocol, and in some variation have been used in virtually every concrete dam since. In 1935 work began on Grand Coulee High Dam in Washington State, and in 1937 on Shasta Dam in Northern California. The principal contractor for Grand Coulee High Dam was Six Companies,[1] which had just finished work at Hoover, and the construction superintendent on Shasta Dam was none other than Frank Crowe.[2]

Shasta impounds the Sacramento River creating Shasta Lake, and Grand Coulee impounds the Columbia River creating Franklin Delano Roosevelt Lake. Both dams were completed and commissioned into service in 1945. Shasta Lake is California's largest man-made reservoir, and Grand Coulee is America's number one producer of hydroelectric power. Although the populations at large in both California and Washington immediately began reaping benefits from the two new dams, their economic success was soon overshadowed by well-publicized outcries over ethnic and ecological damage. Grand Coulee permanently blocked the salmon migration on the Columbia River by removing 1,100 miles of natural spawning habitat, and it also flooded 21,000 acres of sacred, Native American hunting and fishing lands.[3] Like Grand Coulee, Shasta Dam destroyed an important salmon migration from the lower reaches of the Sacramento River, and Shasta Lake inundated the tribal lands of the Winnemem Wintu Indian tribe.[4] As a result of this environmental damage, dam building fell into political disfavor, and resulting new regulations made it much more difficult to build dams.

Shasta Dam itself provides a case in point. Recently, worsening California drought conditions have threatened the vital agricultural output of the California's Central Valley, and discussions about enlarging Shasta Dam have been revived. The BOR has suggested that raising the dam's height by 200 feet to 804 feet would provide a much larger reservoir and a more dependable water supply for irrigation. Agricultural coalitions support the Dam enlargement, but powerful opposition comes from EPA regulations, private environmental groups, and an array of area residents, fisherman, Native Americans, and recreationalists. Though the outcome of the dispute is uncertain, smart money is with the environmentalists.

At 746, 602, and 550 feet high respectively, Hoover, Shasta, and Grand Coulee were the three highest dams in the world from 1945 until 1957, when the Mavoisin Dam in Switzerland surpassed all three at 820 feet. Today US dams are not found among the world's highest and largest. Below is the current list of the world's ten highest dams, along with their country, year completed, and height in feet. Note that none of the great dams is in the Western Hemisphere.

WORLD'S TEN HIGHEST DAMS – 2015

Rank	Building Name	Country	Year Comp.	Height In Feet
1	Jinping I Dam	China	2014	1,001
2	Xiawan Dam	China	2010	958
3	Xiluodu Dam	China	2013	937
4	Grande Dixence Dam	Switzerland	1964	935
5	Inguri Dam	Georgia	1987	891
6	Mavoisin Dam	Switzerland	1957	820
7	Laxiwa Dam	China	2010	820
8	Deriner Dam	Turkey	2012	817
9	Sayano Shushenskaya Dam	Russia	1985	794
10	Ertan Dam	China	1999	790

The ten highest dams in the United States now have an average age of 52 years, and none has been built since 1980. Unless a reasonable balance can somehow be struck between agricultural and environmental interests, it is unlikely that another major dam will ever be built in this country.

SKYSCRAPERS

Beginning in 1908 and continuing for sixty-eight years, the skyscraper was an architectural form pretty much indigenous to the United States. The Woolworth Building, completed in 1913, was the world's tallest building until it was eclipsed by 40 Wall Street in 1930. The Empire State Building wore the crown from April, 1931, until December 23, 1970, when the North Tower of the World Trade Center topped out. The Sears Tower opened in Chicago in 1973, and it would hold the title of world's tallest for twenty-five years. In 1976, First Canadian Place opened in Toronto, Canada and, and suddenly the skyscraper was no longer a uniquely American phenomenon.

In 1990 tall buildings began to pop up in the Eastern Hemisphere. The Bank of China Tower in Hong Kong, at 1,205 feet, was completed in 1990, and Hong Kong became the first of eight countries that would join the skyscraper club before the end of the decade. The other seven were Japan, North Korea, China, Taiwan, Thailand, Malaysia, and the United Arab Emirates. In 1998 the Petronas Towers in Kuala Lumpur, Malaysia topped out at 1,483 feet, and for the first time ever the world's tallest building was not located in the United States. By the end of the millennium only four of the world's ten tallest buildings were in America.

New skyscrapers are proliferating in the 21st century, and most of them are being built in Eastern countries. The Burj Khalifa opened in Dubai in 2010, and is now the world's tallest building with 163 floors and a phenomenal height of 2,717 feet. But its reign will not last long. There are seventeen new skyscrapers currently under construction, and all will be completed by 2020. One of them will surpass the height of Burj Khalifa by more than 500 feet. The Kingdom Tower, now under construction in Jeddah, Saudi Arabia, will reach a dizzying height of 3,280 feet, or exactly one kilometer.[5] At the 2,000 foot level there will be a sky view observation deck which, among other things, will provide magnificent views of the Red Sea. In the rendering below, the observation deck can be seen about half way up on the right side of the building. Ground-breaking for the Kingdom Tower took place on April 1, 2013. Above-ground work commenced in September of 2014, and twenty-five of the planned two-hundred-fifty-two floors have now been completed. When it was conceived, the Kingdom Tower was known as the "Mile High Building," because a height of 5,280 feet was planned. Subsequent engineering studies questioned whether the soil geology under the foundations would support the great weight of such a structure and it was scaled back.

Artist's rendering of Kingdom Tower

At this writing, there are twenty-four buildings taller than the Empire State Building, and seventeen more are under construction. When all are completed, there will be forty-one buildings taller than the Empire State, and only three of them will be located in the United States. This will be the lineup of the world's 10 tallest skyscrapers in 2020.

WORLD'S TEN TALLEST BUILDINGS – 2020

Rank	Building Name	Country	Year Comp.	Height Feet
1	Kingdom Tower	Saudi Arabia	2019*	3,301
2	Burj Khalifa	UAE	2010	2,717
3	Suzhou Zhonghan Center	China	2020*	2,392
4	Ping'an Int'l Finance Center	China	2016*	2,170
5	Signature Tower Ja-karta	Indonesia	2020*	2,093
6	Wuhan Greenland Center	China	2017*	2,087
7	Shanghai Tower	China	2015	2,073
8	KL 118	Malaysia	2019*	2,000
9	Abraj Al-Bait Clock Tower	Saudi Arabia	2012	1,971
10	Goldin Finance 117	China	2016*	1,959

*Under Construction

In the thirty year period from 1990 to 2020, the shift of sky-scraper construction activity from West to East is eye-opening, but it can also be instructive. The shift clearly does not result from any relocation or transplantation of architectural or technological knowhow, as the world's soon-to-be two tallest buildings, Kingdom Tower and Burg Khalifa, were both designed by American architect Adrian Smith of Chicago, Illinois.[6] And most of the world's best structural engineers still either live in or were educated in the United States. So to find the cause of America's decline in skyscraper construction, we must look elsewhere.

LONG SPAN SUSPENSION BRIDGES

The United States pioneered the construction of great suspension bridges, and the work of one man played the key role in establishing American bridge-building pre-eminence. John Augustus Roebling was born in 1806, and studied engineering in his native Prussia in the early nineteenth century. After immigrating to the United States in 1841, he conceived the idea of making wire ropes by twisting bunches of smaller wires together. He believed the wire ropes would be much stronger than traditional hemp ropes, and would be perfect for hauling Canal boats over the Allegheny Mountains. He founded the Roebling & Sons Wire Rope Company to make wire ropes, and soon his Company found itself building suspension bridges.[7]

Mr. Roebling's first major bridge was Cincinnati-Covington Suspension Bridge over the Ohio River, completed in 1867. At the time it was the world's longest suspension bridge, and its name was later changed to the John A. Roebling Suspension Bridge. Roebling and his five sons then designed and built the Brooklyn Bridge (1883) and the George Washington Bridge (1931), and their Company was also the cable contractor for the Golden Gate Bridge (1937). All three bridges continue to be among the world's most famous, and the George Washington still carries more traffic than any other bridge in the world. At its peak before WWII, Roebling & Sons employed more than 8,000 people, and, although the Company was sold after the war, cable-spinning techniques pioneered by the family have been used to build virtually every great suspension bridge in the world. It can literally be said that the Roeblings taught the world how to spin cables.

Until 1973, the world's ten longest suspension bridges were

all located in the United States, and an American bridge would continue to hold the title of world's longest until 1981. The Golden Gate Bridge was the longest for twenty-seven years (1937 to 1964), until the center span of New York's Verrazano Narrows Bridge surpassed it by 60 feet. The Verrazano Narrows wore the crown for seventeen years until it was surpassed by the Humber Bridge in the United Kingdom in 1981. No major suspension bridges have been built in the United States in more than 50 years, and these are the world's ten longest suspension bridges today:

SUSPENSION BRIDGES – WORLD'S 10 LONGEST SPANS

Rank	Building Name	Country	Year Comp.	Height In Feet
1	Akashi Kaikyo Bridge	Japan	1998	6,532
2	Xihoumen Bridge	China	2009	5,413
3	Great Belt Bridge	Denmark	1998	5,328
4	Yi Sun Sin Bridge	S. Korea	2012	5,069
5	Runyang Bridge	China	2005	4,888
6	Nanjing 4th Yangtze Bridge	China	2012	4,652
7	Humber Bridge	UK	1981	4,626
8	Jianquin Bridge	China	1999	4,544
9	Tsing Ma Bridge	Hong Kong	1997	4,518
10	Hardanger Bridge	Norway	2013	4,298

The Akashi Kaikyo bridge has a center span of 6,532 feet, which is about 55% longer than that of the Golden Gate. It is interesting to note, however, that while it took the Japanese ten years to complete the Akashi Kaikyo in 1988, the Golden Gate was completed in a little over four years in 1933. Even without all the advances in bridge-building technology that took place between 1933 and 1978, the Golden Gate Bridge was completed in less than half the time it took for Akashi Kaikyo.

America's four longest suspension bridges today are the Verrazano Narrows, the Golden Gate, the Mackinac, and the George Washington, and they opened to traffic in 1964, 1937, 1957, and 1931, respectively. The four great bridges now have an average age of 68 years.

LARGEST BUILDINGS BY FLOOR SPACE

Nowhere is America's decline in super projects more glaring than in the development of giant, multi-purpose mega-buildings. When the Pentagon was completed in 1953, it was not only the world's largest office building, but also contained more than twice the floor space of any other building in the world, regardless of purpose. The Pentagon's reign as number 1 continued for fifty-three years until 2006 when it was surpassed by Central World in Bangkok, Thailand. Central World is a multi-use complex that includes a shopping mall, a hotel, a convention center, an office complex, public spaces and indoor parking, all under one roof. Central World encloses 11,022,000 square feet of gross leasable floor area ("GLA"), versus the Pentagon's 6,600,000 square feet.

Since the turn of the century twelve new buildings have surpassed the Pentagon in floor area, and only one is in the United States. Six are retail-based, multi-use projects, three are hotel casinos, two are airport terminals, and one, in the Netherlands, is the world's largest flower auction. Below are the current ten largest buildings in the world by floor space.

WORLD'S TEN LARGEST BUILDINGS – 2015

Rank	Building Name	Country	Year Comp.	Square Feet
1	New Century Global Center	China	2013	18,900,000
2	Dubai Int'l Airport Terminal	UAE	2008	18,440,000
3	Abraj Al-Bait Endowment	Saudi Arabia	2012	16,961,930
4	Central World	Thailand	1990	11,020,000
5	Aalsmeer Flower Auction	Netherlands	2008	10,700,000
6	Beijing Int'l Airport Terminal 3	China	2008	10,610,000
7	The Venetian Macau	Macau	2007	10,500,000
8	Sands Cotai Central	Macau	2012	9,600,000
9	Berijaya Times Square	Maylasia	2003	7,500,000
10	Central Park Jakarta Complex	Indonesia	2011	7,100,000

New Century Global Center in Chengdu, China is almost three times as large as the Pentagon.[8] It includes a shopping mall, a university, two commercial office centers, multiple hotels, an Imax Theater, a skating rink, and a giant water park.

A portion of the massive New Century Global Center

The Pentagon remained the largest building in the United States until the Palazzo Hotel opened in Las Vegas in 2007. It still retains the number 2 position domestically.

Of the 50 largest buildings in the world in 2015, only eight are in the United States. With the exception of the Palazzo, all the US structures are more than 23 years old, and their average age is 46 years. Clearly the United States is no longer in the forefront as a developer of world class mega-buildings.

GREAT OCEAN LINERS

Airlines began flying Boeing 707 jet aircraft across the Atlantic in 1958, and from that point forward the days of the great ocean liners were numbered. No more great transatlantic steam ships were built after the SS United States. The great ocean liners had gone the way of the horse and buggy by 1970. SS United States and RMS Queen Mary were both retired from active service in 1967, followed by RMS Queen Elizabeth in 1968. English shipyards later built both a Queen Mary II and a Queen Elizabeth II, but both were diesel powered and both served primarily as cruise ships. No great transatlantic ship ever surpassed the SS United States for speed and safety.

SUMMARY

The United States was the marvel of the architectural and engineering world in 1957 – its unquestioned great builder! The epic projects featured in this book were the most admired and most storied in the world. Not only were they magnificent projects, but they were all built in less time than any others have been before or since. American architects, structural engineers, contractors, and workers of that period were truly masters of the universe.

The world's ten highest dams, ten longest span suspension bridges, ten tallest skyscrapers, and ten largest buildings in 1957 were all located in the United States. Amazingly, one country claimed all forty of the world's greatest man-made structures. But in 1957 the Mavoisin Dam was completed in Switzerland and it displaced Hoover Dam as the world's highest. In 1973 the First Bosphorus Bridge in Istanbul joined the list of top ten bridges, and in 1976 Canada cracked the list of ten tallest skyscrapers with First Canadian Place in Toronto. America's decline continued as Central World opened in Bangkok, Thailand in 1990, with over 11 million square feet of floor space under one roof, almost twice as many as the Pentagon. The United States no longer monopolized the top ten mega-projects in any one major category.

America's slide is now complete. Among the world's ten top dams, long-span suspension bridges, skyscrapers, and largest buildings in 2015, not one is located in the United States. In 58 years, the US has gone from 100% to 0% of the world's forty, foremost structural landmarks. Today's "top forty," are shared by sixteen countries. Nineteen are in China and its "Special Administrative Regions (Macau and Hong Kong)," Saudi Arabia has three, and Switzerland, the United Arab Emirates, Indonesia, and Malaysia have two each. Ten other countries have one each.

So the evidence is clear. The last half of the twentieth century saw a sharp and unmistakable decline in America's preeminence as the world's great builder. We are left to wonder why, and more importantly, whether America can bounce back.

CHAPTER 7

ANALYZING THE DECLINE

"Progress may have been all right once, but
it has gone on too long."

- Ogden Nash

American poet and humorist Ogden Nash made that observation back somewhere in the 1950s. It's doubtful he was referring to epic development projects, but he might just as well have been. His simple musing was prophetic.

The story of America's decline as the world's great builder takes some different twists for different types of projects, but the dam building story provides us with a good metaphor for the overall decline.

A SHORT HISTORY OF AMERICAN DAM BUILDING

Dam builders and engineers in the early twentieth century believed they were advancing American progress. They were taming the savage wilderness by making it acceptable for human settlement. The wild rivers that cut through the Great Plains and the western deserts of the United States had headwaters in major mountain ranges, primarily the Rockies, the Cascades, and the Sierra Nevadas, and flowed uninterrupted from their mountain sources to the Gulf of Mexico or the Pacific. Each Spring enormous quantities of water from snow melt runoffs and Spring rains flooded the land along the rivers, and each summer and fall droughts usually reduced the mighty rivers to mere trickles.

This "feast and famine" pattern of water availability made agriculture, and thus human habitation, virtually impossible. Beginning in the late nineteenth century engineers realized that by building dams at key points along the rivers' natural courses they could create permanent reservoirs, stabilizing the year-round availability of water and making irrigation possible, and dams could also establish renewable sources of affordable hydroelectric power. The BOR, then known as the "United States Reclamation Service," was formed in 1902 to accomplish these worthwhile goals. The BOR's modus operandi was that it would design and engineer the dams, but it would contract with private companies to build them. Today, 180 BOR projects provide water (agricultural, household, & industrial) to 31 million people, irrigate 10 million acres of farmland supplying 60% of the country's vegetables and 25% of its fruits and nuts, and produce a major percentage of the country's renewable hydroelectric power.[1] No reasonable man can argue that BOR has not more than satisfied its original mandates.

But progress requires sacrifice. Notwithstanding its many benefits, dam building, perhaps more than any other type of land and resource development, changes the natural order of things. It indiscriminately floods millions of acres of private and public land, and it adversely impacts the habitats of hundreds of species and varieties of animal and plant life.

The growth of the American environmental movement has closely paralleled the BOR's work, and water development projects have made a perfect target for these groups, The Sierra Club was founded in 1892 by naturalist John Muir, and it was soon followed by the Audobon Society (1905), the National Parks Conservation Association (1919), and the Izaak Walton League (1922). Environmental opposition soon became a major obstacle to any new water project. The environmentalists fought a hard losing battle to stop the Hetch Hetchy Dam in 1912, but were successful in stopping the Echo Park Dam in 1950 and the Bridge Canyon and Marble

Canyon Dams in the early 1960s. The last major authorization for a new BOR project came in the late 1960s. Today there are thirteen major NGO environmental groups with combined memberships of more than 6 million, and they zealously and vocally guide and support the efforts of the US Environmental Agency (EPA), an independent US regulatory agency formed in 1970 with cabinet level authority.

The environmental movement today is seeking to decommission the huge Glen Canyon Dam in Northern Arizona and drain Lake Powell.[2] It has also targeted four major dams on the Lower Snake River in Eastern Washington for decommissioning. The BOR, for its part, no longer considers "construction" as part of its responsibilities, and has narrowed its official mandate to "manage, develop, and protect water and related resources in an environmentally and economically sound manner in the interest of the American public."[3] The EPA has become America's number 1 regulator. The Competitive Enterprise Institute estimates that the title "Environment Protection" in the US Code of Federal Regulations contains 88,852 specific environmental regulations. Just since 2009 the EPA has issued 2,827 final regulations, consuming 24,915 pages of the Federal Register and almost 25 million words.

Today, the US Government owns 58% of all the land in eleven Western states, a land mass comprising almost one million square miles.[4] By wielding its weapon of regulation, it effectively prohibits any development on this massive expanse of real estate. The State of California is currently suffering through its worst drought in recent history, and it has not built a new reservoir in more than thirty-five years. The life-threatening water shortages in the State have given rise to numerous proposals for new dams and enlargement of existing dams, but these proposals are largely falling on deaf ears and stand little chance against the powerful armies of the federal government and environmental movement.

Henry David Thoreau, perhaps America's first and certainly one of its most revered environmentalists, wrote these words in 1848 in his famous essay "On the Duty of Civil Disobedience:" [5]

> *"That government is best which governs least."*
>
> *- Henry David Thoreau*

Thoreau would not like where things are today.

BIG GOVERNMENT & EXPLODING REGULATION

> *"Individual freedom and the profit motive were the engines of progress which transformed an American wilderness into an economic dynamo that provided the American people with a standard of living that is still the envy of the world"*[6]
>
> *- Ronald Reagan*

Many of those who ponder over man's ability to govern himself identify the writing of the American founding documents in 1776 and 1787 as history's high water mark. Its new Constitution established the United States of America as a constitutional republic. A republic is not a democracy. It is a system wherein decisions are not made by a majority vote of the people, but rather by representatives of the people, freely and periodically elected by them to act within the framework of a written constitution. Before taking office, the President and all the people's elected representatives take an oath swearing to "preserve, protect, and defend the Constitution" (in the case of the President) or to "support and defend the Constitution" (in the case of Congress).

When George Washington took the Presidential oath in 1789, four cabinet-level departments were established to conduct the government's business. They were the Departments of State, Treasury, War (now Defense) and the Attorney General (now Justice). At the end of his second term in office in 1809, President Thomas Jefferson's executive staff consisted of a total of seventeen employees.[7] The federal government was small and efficient back then by anyone's standard. But no more.

Today the US has fifteen cabinet-level departments, seven of them established since 1953. Together, they employ almost one million people and spend one and one-half trillion dollars annually.[8] In addition to cabinet departments, the country has an estimated 2,000 "government corporations," "independent agencies," and "regulatory agencies." A few examples are the US Post Office, Amtrak, NASA, the Securities and Exchange Commission, the Federal Reserve System, and the EPA. In total, the United States now has more than 20 million public employees doing its business, and approximately 35% of them are union members.[9] Public union members are paid an average of 10% to 30% more than non-union workers for the same jobs. These bloated wage rates and the union membership growth rates both exceed those of non-union employees because a) union wages and working conditions are negotiated with elected public officials who are spending taxpayer money, and not their own b) union political power influences public officials in negotiations c) local governments, unlike businesses, cannot threaten to move elsewhere, and d) local governments, unlike businesses, face no outside competition.

In addition to the cabinet departments and public agencies, thousands of "NGOs" (non-government organizations) have been formed to promote special interests and lobby elected officials for political support.

This vast government bureaucracy "regulates" the private sector. It churns out new regulations at an alarming rate. At the end of 2013, the Code of Federal Regulations contained an estimated 175 million words that filled up 235 volumes. The index alone was 1,170 pages long.[10] For the sake of comparison, The Declaration of Independence and the US Constitution contain 1,458 and 4,534 words, respectively.

The National Association of Manufacturers (NAM) estimates that the private sector in this country spends in excess of $2 trillion annually on compliance with the mountain of federal regulations.

"The natural progress of things is for liberty to yield and government to gain ground. Even under the best forms of government, those entrusted with power have, in time and by slow operations, perverted it into tyranny."

- Thomas Jefferson

America's decline not only as the world's great builder, but its decline generally results in no small part from an explosion in the growth of government regulation and bureaucracy, which suffocates innovation, accomplishment, and exceptionalism. Government regulation and free enterprise capitalism are antithetical, and excessive regulation will always drive away the flow of human commerce.

In 1994, after earthquakes destroyed major Los Angeles freeways, then-California Governor Pete Wilson did what politicians always do, he declared a state of emergency. But he also did one more thing, not so ordinary. Fully understanding the monumental repair job that lay ahead in the country's most heavily regulated state, the Governor called for a one-time waiver of all highway repair regulations, and authorized financial incentives for all contractors who agreed to complete repairs by a date certain. As a result, the Santa Monica Freeway was rebuilt to a higher standard than before the earthquakes in just 66 days.[11] This event represented a rare admission by a political bureaucrat that regulations do not help but hinder progress, and it also revealed the well-kept secret that, contrary to what they might say, all politicians know it.

Domestic development has slowed to a virtual crawl due to the unbridled growth of government and regulation. Both people and capital are now very mobile, and will seek out venues where their projects can be planned, designed, permitted and built in a reasonable period of time. With veritable armies of attorneys, engineers, and consultants now required to navigate the construction permitting processes in the United States, enormous, non-productive costs are generated that simply cannot be amortized over a project's economic life. So people, capital, and projects are going elsewhere. America is simply no longer competitive when it comes to major development projects.

CULTURAL DECAY – ENTITLEMENT & DEPENDENCE

"When government accepts responsibility for people, then people no longer accept responsibility for themselves."

- George Pataki

In 1976 British diplomat and historian Sir John Glubb wrote a book called "The Fate of Empires and Search for Survival."[12] In his book Glubb analyzes the eleven greatest nation states the world has known since 1,000 BC. He calculates that the life spans of the great nation states ranged from 208 years to 267 years, and that the average span was 250 years. Glubb believes that all eleven empires went through the same six distinct periods or ages; the ages of pioneers, conquest, commerce, affluence, intellect, and decadence.

Dated from the Declaration of Independence, the United States is now 239 years old, and according to timelines established in Glubb's work, is in its age of decadence, or cultural decay. He believes decadence results from a too-long period of wealth and power, selfishness, love of money, and loss of a sense of duty. Glubb notes that the features which characterize the age of decadence, are pessimism, materialism, an influx of immigrants, the welfare state (entitlement), and the weakening of religion.[13] If two more features could be added, Glubb's definition of decadence would almost perfectly mirror conditions in 2015 America. First is a precipitous decline in the quality of education, and second is the abandonment of the country's founding principles by its government. We now live in a society in which our schools refuse to teach the very civic values that have been proven to strengthen and protect it from enemies seeking to destroy it, and one in which elected officials repeatedly violate their oaths of office by subverting rather than defending the Constitution.

Public opinion in America is driven today by a noisy, radical minority which is strongly pro-government and which has no apparent loyalty to the values and institutions that built the country. This group promotes victimhood, class warfare, entitlements, and "social justice," and it rails against capitalism, Christianity, the Constitution, self reliance, American exceptionalism, and the US military establishment. Although still a minority, the group makes itself seem much larger than it is by using the social media as a megaphone to spread its ideas. The group has the enthusiastic support of the public education establishment, the movie and music industries, the mainstream media, and the Democrat party.

Many Americans refer to this radical minority as the "Entitlement Society," or simply as the "radical left." In 1991 forty-one million American households received some form means-tested entitlements, which include food stamps, unemployment insurance, subsidized housing, federal disability, and welfare payments. Twenty-one years later, in 2012, that number had swollen to one-hundred-seven million households, an increase of 161%. In 1992, 23 million Americans used food stamps, and today the number is over 46 million. Three and one-half million people received federal disability payments back then, compared with nine million today. Perhaps most shocking of all, the United States now has over 93 million adults who do not participate in the work force.[14] No matter how it is spun, sliced or massaged, that number means that more than 41% of the country's entire adult population does not choose to work and is dependent on someone or something other than his own labors for sustenance.

The American Founding Fathers were well aware that vote buying via entitlement payments could ultimately destroy their noble experiment at self-government, and they tried hard to write language into their new Constitution that not only discouraged but prohibited entitlement payments. But almost before the ink was dry on their document there were "rats in the corn crib," and a drift away from Constitutional principles had begun.

Benjamin Franklin, the elder statesman among the Founding Fathers, made this prescient observation on entitlements:

"I am for doing good to the poor, but...I think the best way of doing good to the poor, is not making them easy in poverty, but leading or driving them out of it. I observed...that the more public provisions were made for the poor, the less they provided for themselves, and of course became poorer. And, on the contrary, the less was done for them, the more they did for themselves, and became richer."

— Benjamin Franklin

The purpose of politicians who promise entitlements to their constituents is not to improve their lots in life, but rather to buy their votes. Franklin and his compatriots fully understood that entitlements sap the motivation and destroy the ambition of recipients, which explains today's oft-repeated claim that this country must welcome immigrant workers, legal and illegal, to fill jobs that "Americans just won't do." Growing numbers of otherwise qualified Americans will not do any job, simply because entitlements have replaced ambition.

One can only wonder whether those great men who built Hoover Dam, the Golden Gate Bridge, the Empire State Building and the Pentagon so many years ago would have been able to work their way through today's vast regulatory maze, and whether they could have assembled an ambitious, motivated and effective work force in today's entitled America.

AMERICA BY THE NUMBERS – 2015

At the time it was created in 1787, the American Constitutional Republic was viewed by the rest of the world as an experiment. Not even the framers themselves were convinced that their new republic would last. But last it did. For over 200 years, the American system of representative government, of the people, by the people and for the people, was the marvel and the envy of the world. But decades of cultural decay have taken a terrible toll on the Republic, and now threaten its very foundations. Doubters need only look at the numbers.

- *The U.S. national debt stands at $18.180 trillion, which is more than twice the 2007 amount and 50 times the 1970 level, and which for the first time in history exceeds the country's gross domestic product (GDP),15*

- *Over the past ten years, the United States government has spent morethan it has collected by an average of more than $1 trillion per year,16*

- *The total US work force today is 148 million, 5 million smaller than it wasin 2000,15*

- *Today, 93 million Americans do not participate in the workforce, 15 million more than in 2000,*

- *Median income today is $29,000, exactly the same as it was in 2000, whilethe median price of a new home has risen from $171,000 to $282,000,15*

- *Forty-six million Americans receive food stamps, 44 million live in poverty,*

- *41 million do not have insurance, and 159 million receive some type of entitlement,15*

- *The actual "U-6" unemployment rate (unemployed and under-employed) is 11.5% of the work force,15 and Only 46% of American children live in two-parent homes, compared with 73% in 1960 17*

Despite the looming possibility of total economic collapse, American political leaders in both parties ignore these numbers. Growing deficits and out-of-control-federal spending are seldom discussed during television talk shows and political campaigns, presumably out of fear of creating public panic. While they paper over these obvious problems, our leaders continue to pursue the same, failed policies that have brought us to edge of the abyss. The spreading cancers of regulation and entitlement continue to paralyze economic growth, and default is staved off only by the debasement of the currency. And through all this turmoil the United States continues to be the only country in the world that stubbornly refuses to develop its own natural resources in order to pay its debts and advance its standard of living.

Many scholars regard the United States Constitution as the greatest primary governing document ever written, but the period since 1950 has been marked by an accelerating drift away from the principles set forth in that great document, and today's America is crippled by big-government bureaucracy, over-regulation, entitlement, and dependency.

More and more Americans seem to finally be realizing that something is seriously wrong with their country, and are beginning to long for the unity and prosperity that they believe will result from a return to Constitutional principles. Is it too late, and is the march toward mediocrity and oblivion irreversible, or can America still bounce back?

CHAPTER 8

CAN AMERICA BOUNCE BACK?

Sir John Glubb studied Assyria, 859 – 612 BC, Persia, 538 – 330 BC, Greece, 331 – 100 BC, the Roman Republic, 260 – 27 BC, the Roman Empire, 27 BC – 180 AD, the Arab Empire, 634 – 880, the Mameluke Empire (Egypt), 1250 – 1517, the Ottoman Empire, 1320 – 1570, Spain, 1500 – 2750, Romanov Russia, 1682 – 1916, and Great Britain, 1700 – 1950 . None of these eleven great societies was ever able to bounce back and reverse its slide from decadence into oblivion, although undoubtedly their more enlightened members would have tried.

"Saving us from the fate of other great empires will require a revival of the American spirit and a renewal of our faith in the values and institutions that made us great."

- Cal Thomas

Cal Thomas is undoubtedly correct, but even with a revived spirit and renewed faith how can America reverse the slide and bounce back? Logic dictates that the things that caused the slide must be reversed or eliminated. That means regulations must be rolled back, entitlement programs must be eliminated, and government growth must be reversed. Are those things possible, and if so how can they be brought about? Let's explore some possibilities.

THE ELECTORAL PROCESS

When politicians make bad decisions and the wheels of progress come off the tracks, Americans believe they need only wait until the next election. Then, assuming the majority of voters will share their views, they will simply "throw the bums out," and things will return to normal. But lately, that simple ballot box fix doesn't seem to be working.

Unfortunately, America's downward spiral has now reached a point where it is virtually impossible to stop it at the ballot box. Government entitlements have spread like a cancer throughout American households until a majority of voters are now dependent upon one or more forms of federal largesse to maintain their lifestyles. Jeff Thomas writes regularly for the Casey publication "International Man," and Jeff says that, no matter how much flag waving they might do, Americans will never willingly give up their entitlements.[1] Jeff is probably right.

A few years ago, we don't know exactly when, the United States quietly and without fanfare reached a tipping point, when for the first time in history more voters were net recipients of federal money than were paying into the system. There were suddenly more takers than givers. The more the givers pay, the more there is for the taking. Since that tipping point was reached, there is no turning back, and no solution at the polls. In today's political environment, any presidential candidate who advocates for lower taxes and reduced entitlements is probably wasting his time and his campaign funds.

So, if real change can no longer be effected through the electoral process, then how?

A SEMINAL, GAME-CHANGING CATASTROPHE

"There are no atheists in foxholes, and there are no ideologues in a financial crisis."

- Ben Bernanke

James Rickards is a best-selling author, widely-respected monetary expert, and student of complexity theory. Rickards and a growing number of his fellow economists believe a catastrophic collapse of United States financial markets is a virtual certainty in the near future. According to the science of complexity theory, "complex" systems differentiate themselves from all other systems by having unique characteristics; they arise spontaneously, they behave unpredictably, they exhaust resources, and they collapse catastrophically.[2] The world's system of capital markets is a complex system nonpareil. It consists of millions of investors, traders, speculators, brokers, exchanges, trading platforms and institutions, many employing high frequency trading and investment algorithms, all of them interdependent. Risk in complex systems is exponential. That means that when the size of the system doubles, risk increases by 10 X, and when it double again, by 100 X.[3]

Rickards believes financial markets are in a critical state, and he recently published a list of thirty possible "triggering events," any of which could ignite a collapse.[4] Once it starts, cascades of sell orders will hit one or more markets without any bids. In a matter of minutes fortunes will evaporate, and contagion will spread rapidly. Banks will fail, and sovereign governments will be bankrupt.

The kind of financial collapse envisioned by Rickards and his colleagues will be a seminal, game-changing event for the United States. Decisions the sitting government makes in the aftermath of a collapse, and the reaction of the populace to those decisions, will likely set the nation's course for generations to come.

A brief review of the country's founding concepts and principles will be helpful as we explore possibilities.

THE SOCIAL CONTRACT

The concept of a social contract forms the primary bedrock of the American political system. The origin of the term dates back to Plato in ancient Greece, but as used today the social contract is a theory developed in Western Europe during the Age of Enlightenment (1650 to 1780). Thomas Hobbes, John Locke, Jean Jacques Rousseau and Immanuel Kant are the most prominent advocates of social contract political theory, and John Locke in particular had a great influence on America's Founding Fathers, particularly on Alexander Hamilton, James Madison and Thomas Jefferson.[5] Jefferson wrote *"Bacon, Locke, and Newton... I consider them the three greatest men who have ever lived, without any exception..."*

Locke believed that natural rights were inalienable, and that the rule of God superseded the authority of any government. In a social contract, the citizens would agree to obey and support the government in exchange for government's promise to secure and protect the natural rights of its citizens. He believed that if and when a government failed to protect the rights of its citizens, then the social contract was broken, and the citizens' obligations to it ended. The citizens could alter or abolish the government by elections or other means including, when necessary, violence.

Locke's influence on the authors of America's Founding documents was profound and is apparent in much of the language in both documents. Scholars believe the phrase "life, liberty, and the pursuit of happiness," in the Declaration was probably borrowed from Locke's assertion that "Every man has a natural right to defend his life, health, liberty and possessions," and one of Locke's phrases "long train of abuses," is used verbatim in the Declaration.

"We the people," the Constitution's first three words, mirror Locke's idea of popular sovereignty, and the second paragraph of the Declaration of Independence, below, closely mimics Locke's views on rights and revolution.

"We hold these truths to be self-evident, that all men are created equal, that they are endowed by their Creator with certain unalienable Rights,

that among these are Life, Liberty, and the pursuit of Happiness.—That to secure these rights, Governments are instituted among Men, deriving their just powers from the consent of the governed, -- That whenever any form of Government becomes destructive of these ends, it is the Right of the People to alter or to abolish it, and to institute a new Government,

laying its foundations on such principles and organizing its powers in such form, as to them shall seem most likely to effect their Safety and Happiness."

Thomas Jefferson, July 4, 1776

Many Americans have not studied nor even read either the Declaration of Independence or the US Constitution, because "non-revisionist" American History is no longer taught in most public schools. Consequently, many do not realize that the founding documents provide them the means to remove from office those elected representatives who either abuse their powers or who violate their oaths of office.

Although Presidents and Congressmen are aware of the remedies available to the people, most have impugned the provisions of the Constitution for decades without voter reprisal, and thus believe that their poorly-informed constituents regard the US Constitution as a dead letter. But the Social Contract has been broken, and that is important to whatever comes next. If the Republic is to be saved, the people must act. As Irish statesman and political philosopher Edmund Burke wrote:

"The only thing necessary for the triumph of evil is for good men to do nothing."

Jefferson's words from the Declaration still ring loud and clear, and should remind all once again that elected officials derive their powers from the consent of the governed. If that consent is withdrawn, either by ballot or by the operation of law, then they no longer have power. If abuses are serious enough, the people have redress through their right to abolish the government. Though it is much maligned, the Constitution remains the law of the land, and it requires a government of the people, by the people, and for the people.

"Freedom is never more than one generation away from extinction. We didn't pass it to our children in the bloodstream. It must be fought for, protected, and handed on for them to do the same, or one day we will spend our sunset years telling our children and our children's children what it was once like in the United States where men were free."

Ronald Reagan

A PROBABLE GOVERNMENTAL REACTION TO ARMAGEDDON

To any government, retaining power when under siege totally overwhelms all other instincts, so normally, its first act in any crisis is to declare a "state of emergency." According to Wikipedia, a state of emergency is "a governmental declaration giving it the power to suspend or change functions of the executive, legislative, and judicial branches for a given period of time. It can also be used as a rationale for suspending rights and freedoms guaranteed to the governed under the Constitution."[6]

In financial emergencies, capital flight will be one of Government's biggest fears, and Washington can be expected to impose some combination of the following draconian "capital controls."

146

- <u>International Travel and Customs Restrictions to Prevent Capital Flight</u> – Strict restrictions will be imposed on the amounts of cash and the types of assets that international travelers can legally carry.

- <u>Imposition of Martial Law and Curfews</u> – To discourage civil violence and protest, the Government will impose curfews and martial law.

- <u>Bank Holidays, Confiscation of Deposits, and Withdrawal Restrictions to Protect Banks</u> - In 1934 FDR declared a "Bank Holiday," to give Government time to develop a plan to save the banks. If the banks are allowed to remain open, onerous limits will be placed on withdrawals and wire transfers will be suspended. New law enables banks to simply confiscate deposits via "bail-ins."

- <u>Confiscation of Privately Owned Gold and Silver</u> – President Roosevelt took this step in 1933, when he issued Executive Order 6102.[7] Those who surrendered their precious metals were compensated, but at far less than the then-prevailing market values.

- <u>Nationalization of Retirement Accounts and/or a One-off Wealth Tax</u> - It is estimated that the total value of all US IRAs, 401-Ks and other retirement accounts approaches $20 trillion, and Washington could redirect these investments into Government bonds. The International Monetary Fund is on record as advocating a one-off tax on wealth instead of income.

- <u>Temporary or Permanent Suspension of Entitlement Transfer Payments</u> – Under the protective cloak of a "National Emergency" the Government could suspend funding for food stamps, unemployment compensation, and disability and welfare payments.

There are limits and restraints upon the President in his exercise of emergency powers. With the exception of the habeas corpus clause, the Constitution makes no allowance for the suspension of any of its provisions during a national emergency. Disputes over the constitutionality or legality of the exercise of emergency powers are judicially reviewable. Indeed, both the judiciary and Congress, as co-equal branches, can restrain the executive regarding emergency powers, and so can public opinion. Many measures enacted by President Roosevelt during the Great Depression were overturned by the Supreme Court, and resulted in his failed attempt to "pack the Court." [8]

As we have shown, the social contract obligates the government to protect the rights of its citizens. Capital controls, however, clearly protect government to the detriment of its citizens, and the measures suggested above would constitute additional violations of the social contract.

A catastrophic economic collapse would trigger a constitutional crisis, bringing American citizens face to face an with an overwhelmingly important decision: In an emergency will they acquiesce to unconstitutional, authoritarian government edicts, or will they exercise their Rights under their county's founding documents "to alter or abolish the government, and to institute a new one, laying its foundations on such principles and organizing its powers in such form, as to them shall seem most likely to effect their safety and happiness."

A BLOODLESS REVOLUTION

*"In a crisis, be aware of the danger – but recognize
the opportunity."*

- John Fitzgerald Kennedy

If the government reacts as history suggests it will, it is not possible to know exactly what impact its reaction will have on disparate segments of society. The productive, taxpaying segment of the population will have little patience with an oppressive, authoritarian government, and unconstitutional, emergency measures can be expected to generate widespread anger and antipathy against Washington. The unemployed, "entitled" segment of society, for its part, will likely use the crisis as just another reason to take to the streets, as it has recently been doing with little provocation. Chaos will likely reign for some period of time until recovery can begin, and, as Kennedy points out, with chaos comes opportunity.

In the superheated political aftermath of a catastrophic event like the one we expect, could a well-organized opposition form a coalition to challenge the legitimacy of a sitting government? Could a group of modern-day "Founding Fathers," dedicated to re-establishing the Constitution as the law of the land, assemble its own legion of twenty-first century minutemen and effect a rebirth of American greatness by deposing leaders in the executive branch of the government? The rationale for such an insurgency, just as it was back in July of 1776, would be to end the "long train of abuses and usurpations" perpetrated by sitting governments against the Constitution of the United States, and the breach of the social contract between government and governed.

Historically, the forceful seizure of a country's key government offices without changing its underlying system of government is known as a Coup d'Etat.[9] For a Coup d'Etat to succeed in the United States, the support of the country's armed forces would be essential. But with that armed support, a successful overthrow and takeover would be virtually assured.

Glubb observed in the *History of Empires and Search for Survival,* that "decadence is the disintegration of a system, and not of its individual members."[10] He believed his research proved that the decline of any nation does not undermine the basic character of its members, and that when members of a society are introduced into new surroundings and are enabled to break away from their old channels of thought, that after a short period of readjustment they become normal citizens in their new environment.

Applied to today's American dilemma, Glubb's research would seem to confirm that once a new course is embarked upon, all Americans could over time abandon their old ideas and embrace a rebirth of Constitutional government and exceptionalism.

THE KEY TO SUCCESS – UNCOMMON MEN

Perhaps more important than the success of the insurrection itself would be the ability of its leaders to fully restore constitutional governance and to institute changes that would prevent a recurrence of the steady drift away from the Constitution that has plagued the country's first 228 years. The most important determinant of a successful Coup, just as it was with the American Revolution itself, will be the quality of the men who lead it.

"The history of the world is but the biography of great men."

- Thomas Carlyle

America was founded by great men, and throughout its history has produced more than its share. With the exception of

James Madison, the Founding Fathers were not career politicians. Washington, Jefferson and Monroe were farmers, Adams and Hamilton were lawyers, and of course Franklin was a scientist, inventor, and entrepreneur. Four were from Virginia, one from Massachusetts, one from Pennsylvania, and one was an orphan from the West Indies. These seven great men were pulled together not by friendship but by a common cause, that of designing a way to govern themselves and their fellow citizens. We know, of course, that they succeeded, and in doing so changed the world.

In literature, great men are often said to "possess the pioneering spirit," or they are referred to as "adventurers," or "heroes." Whatever they are called, such men are uncommon, and represent an extremely small percentage of any population. When facing new challenges, great men instinctively know what to do, without reasoning or analysis.

Those who built the great projects featured in this book were great men. They all valued liberty and self reliance, and they hated all bureaucracy and regulation. They all viewed government not as a partner, but as a necessary evil to be avoided whenever possible.

Even though the US Government provided half the financing for the SS United States, for Willam Francis Gibbs, the ship was never the result of a partnership between private business and the government. For him, not money, but the ship's design and construction created SS United States, and for him, creativity came out of a team, never a bureaucracy. He said later,

"The reason we managed to construct this great ship that lies up at Pier 86 was that the government left us to ourselves, putting no regulations in our way..."

After Gibbs died his Chief Engineer, Walter Bachman said that

"Even as he aged, Gibbs was a natural born leader, who inspired great loyalty in his staff and confidence and cooperation among all those with whom he did business."

Brehon Burke Somervell fought a life-long, every day battle against bureaucracy.[11]Everyone who worked for him knew that the fastest way to get fired was to blame a delay on paperwork. General George C. Marshall was variously Chief of Staff of the US Army, US Secretary of Defense, and US Secretary of State. He was one of only ten US military officers to ever be awarded five star rank, and he also was awarded the Nobel Prize for Peace. When asked what he would do if he were ever put in charge of another global war, General Marshall did not hesitate.

"I would start out looking for another General Somervell the very first thing I did, and so would anybody else who went through World war II on his side."[12]

Frank Crowe was nicknamed "Hurry Up Crowe," by those who worked for him, but he had his critics, one of whom said,

"Crowe's defining trademark was his relentless demand for progress. Certainly nothing in the contract, the construction schedule, or the elements mandated such haste. The phenomenal pace of the job just seemed be a point of pride with Crowe."

The critic totally missed the point. Of course that trait was a point of pride with Crowe, and more important, it was the primary reason for his greatness. At the end of World War II, when the government was looking for one great man to oversee the huge job of rebuilding Europe, the first man it turned to was a dam builder from Maine, Frank Crowe.

CONCLUSION

We have outlined only one hypothetical path that events

might take as America continues its retreat from exceptionalism, but it is one that might stop the slide. How events actually will unfold for the country going forward is anyone's guess, for none of us can see into the future with clarity. We have suggested that America's malaise will end soon with one game-changing, seminal event. We hope it does. If it does, and if we should ever be asked what could be done to bring about a rebirth of America, we would follow General Marshall's advice.

We would go looking for another Somervell, another Crowe, another Gibbs, Starrett and Roebling; another group of founding fathers. In the 1860s Poet Walt Whitman watched as a great man named Abraham Lincoln struggled mightily to save the Union from collapse. Whitman memorialized Lincoln's death with his moving poem "Oh Captain, my Captain,"[13] and he left us all with this enduring advice –

"Produce great men, and the rest will follow."

NOTES

1. HOOVER DAM

1. Joseph E. Stevens, *Hoover Dam: An American Adventure.* (Norman, OK: University of Oklahoma Press, 1988) 10.

2. Michael A. Hiltzik, *Colossus: Hoover Dam and the Making of the American Century* (New York: Free Press, 2010) 30

3. Hiltzik, *Colossus: Hoover Dam and the Making of the American Century*, 42.

4. ibid. 81-87.

5. Dennis McBride, "Frank Crowe" *Las Vegas Review Journal, Feb 7, 1999* http://www.reviewjournal.com/news/frank-crowe ibid.

6. Christy Barth, *Masters of Mass Production* (Indianapolis: Bobbs-Merrill Co., 1945) 118- 120.

7. McBride, "Frank Crowe" http://www.reviewjournal.com/news/frank-crowe

8. "Historic Construction Projects – Hoover Dam" http://www.generalcontractor.com/resources/articles/hoover-dam.asp

9. ibid.

10. "Frank Crowe . Hoover Dam" *PBS American Experience* http://www.pbs.org/wgbh/americanexperience/features/biography/hoover-crowe/

11. Hiltzik, *Colossus: Hoover Dam and the Making of the American Century*, 120.

12. Stevens, *Hoover Dam: An American Adventure*, 34.

13. "Historic Construction Projects – Hoover Dam"
http://www.generalcontractor.com/resources/articles/ho
over-dam.asp

14. Stevens, *Hoover Dam: An American Adventure,* 35-42.

15. Hiltzic, *Colossus: Hoover Dam and the Making of the American Century,* 172-178

16. ibid. 175

17. "Historic Construction Projects – Hoover Dam"
http://www.generalcontractor.com/resources/articles/ho
over-dam.asp

18. Andrew J.Dunar and Dennis J. Mcbride, *Building Hoover Dam: An Oral History of the   Great Depression.* (Reno: University of Nevada Press, 2001) 40.

19. "Historic Construction Projects – Hoover Dam"
http://www.generalcontractor.com/resources/articles/ho
over-dam.asp

20. Hiltzic, *Colossus: Hoover Dam and the Making of the American Century,* 33.

21. ibid.

22. ibid.

23. "Historic Construction Projects – Hoover Dam"
http://www.generalcontractor.com/resources/articles/ho
over-dam.asp

24. Hiltzic, *Colossus: Hoover Dam and the Making of the American Century,* 290.

25. ibid. 305-306.

26. "Historic Construction Projects – Hoover Dam"
http://www.generalcontractor.com/resources/articles/ho

over-dam.asp

27. Stevens, *Hoover Dam: An American Adventure*, 35-42.

28. Hoover Dam, Wikipedia
http://en.wikipedia.org/wiki/Hoover_Dam

29. Hiltzic, *Colossus: Hoover Dam and the Making of the American Century*, 331-332.

30. ibid. 326.

31. ibid. 329.

32. ibid. 346

33. Bureau of Reclamation *Lower Colorado Region – Hoover Power FAQs*
http://www.usbr.gov/lc/hooverdam/faqs/powerfaq.html

34. ibid.

35. Hiltzic, *Colossus: Hoover Dam and the Making of the American Century*, 346.

36. ibid. 333

37. "Historic Construction Projects – Hoover Dam"
http://www.generalcontractor.com/resources/articles/ho over-dam.asp

38. ibid.

39. Bureau of Reclamation *Lower Colorado Region – Hoover Power FAQs*
http://www.usbr.gov/lc/hooverdam/faqs/powerfaq.html

40. ibid.

41. Hiltzic, *Colossus: Hoover Dam and the Making of the American Century*, 408.

42. McBride, "Frank Crowe"
    http://www.reviewjournal.com/news/frank-crowe

43. Hiltzic, *Colossus: Hoover Dam and the Making of the American Century*,

44. "Frank Crowe . Hoover Dam" *PBS American Experience*
    http://www.pbs.org/wgbh/americanexperience/features/
    biography/hoover-crowe/

45. ibid.

46. McBride, "Frank Crowe"
    http://www.reviewjournal.com/news/frank-crowe

47. "Frank Crowe . Hoover Dam" *PBS American Experience*
    http://www.pbs.org/wgbh/americanexperience/fe
    atures/biography/hoover-crowe/

48. Hiltzic, *Colossus: Hoover Dam and the Making of the American Century*, 407.

49. ibid.

50. ibid.

51. *The Hoover Dam – Ten Top Public Works Projects of the Century.*
    http://www2.apwa.net/about/awards/toptencentury/hoo
    v.htm

2. THE GOLDEN GATE BRIDGE

1. Pete Sigmund, The Golden Gate Bridge: The Bridge That
    Couldn't Be Built, Construction Equipment Guide,
    http://www.constructionequipmentguide.com/historical/g
    olden-gate-   bridge/

2. Peter Fimrite, Ferry Tale –The Dream Dies Hard: 2 Historic
    Boats that Plied the Bay Seek Buyer – Anybody, San Fran-

cisco Chronicle , April 28, 2005
http://www.sfgate.com/cgibin/article.cgi?f=/c/a2005/04/28/BAG8BCGI3Il.DTL&hw=ferr y&sn=310&sc=862

3. Golden Gate Bridge, United States History.com
http://www.u-s-history/pages/h2576.html

4. ibid.

5. Joseph Strauss . Golden Gate Bridge . WGBH American Experience | PBS http://www.pbs.org/wgbh/american experience/features/biography/goldengate-strauss/

6. People & Events . Joseph Strauss (1870-1938) WGBH American Experience | PBS
http://www.pbs.org/wgbh/amex/goldengate/peopleevents/p_strauss.html

7. Golden Gate Bridge, United States History.com
http://www.u-s-history/pages/h2576.html

8. ibid.

9. John B. Miller, Case Studies in Infrastructure Delivery, (Springer 2002)

10. Golden Gate Bridge, United States History.com
http://www.u-s-history/pages/h2576.html

11. Pete Sigmund, The Golden Gate Bridge: The Bridge That Couldn't Be Built

12. People & Events . Joseph Strauss (1870-1938) WGBH American Experience | P

13. Golden Gate Bridge, United States History.com
http://www.u-s-history/pages/h2576.html

14. ibid.

15. Charles Ellis . Golden Gate Bridge. WGBH American Experi-

ence | PBS
http://www.pbs.org/wgbh/americanexperience/features/
biography/goldengate-ellis/

16. ibid.

17. ibid.

18. ibid.

19. ibid.

20. Pete Sigmund, The Golden Gate Bridge: The Bridge That Couldn't Be Built

21. Amadeo Gianini . Golden Gate Bridge. WGBH American Experience | PBS

22. http://www.pbs.org/wgbh/americanexperience/features/
biography/goldengate-gianini/

23. ibid.

24. Stephen Cassady, Spanning the Gate. (Mill Valley, CA, Squarebooks, 1979) 36

25. Amy Standen, Life and the Gate: Working on the Golden Gate Bridge 1933 – 37, Quest   Northern California
http://science.kqed.org/quest/audio.life-on-the-gate-working-on-the-golden-gate-bridge-   1933-37/

26. ibid.

27. Underwater Construction . WGBH American Experience | PBS
http://www.pbs.org/wgbh/americanexperience/features/
general-article/goldengate-   underwater/

28. ibid.

29. ibid.

30. Golden Gate Bridge,
    http://goldegatebridge.org/research/factsGGBDesign.php

31. Spinning the Cables . Golden Gate Bridge .WGBH American
    Experience | PBS

32. http://www.pbs.org/wgbh/americanexperience/features/
    general-article/goldengate-   spinning/

33. ibid.

34. Stephen Cassady, Spanning the Gate. (Mill Valley, CA,
    Squarebooks, 1979) 84.

35. Spinning the Cables . Golden Gate Bridge .WGBH American
    Experience | PBS

36. ibid.

37. Stephen Cassady, Spanning the Gate. (Mill Valley, CA,
    Squarebooks, 1979) 103.

38. Golden Gate Bridge,
    http://goldegatebridge.org/research/factsGGBDesign.php

39. Joseph Strauss . Golden Gate Bridge . WGBH American Ex-
    perience | PBS

40. Golden Gate Bridge, United States History.com

41. Golden Gate Bridge,
    http://goldegatebridge.org/tolls_traffic/

42. Golden Gate Bridge: Research Library: How Often is the
    Golden Gate Bridge   Repainted?" Golden Gate Bridge,
    Highway and Transportation District. (2006)
    http://goldengatebridge.org/research/facts.php

43. Joseph Strauss . Golden Gate Bridge . WGBH American Ex-
    perience |

44. Charles Ellis . Golden Gate Bridge. WGBH American Experience | PBS

45. American Society of Civil Engineers Seven Wonders http://www.asce.org/Content.aspx?id=2147487305

3. MANHATTAN SKYSCRAPERS & THE EMPIRE STATE BUIDLING

1. Ed Grabianowski, *Empire State Building Completed – How Stuff Works*, http://science.howstuffworks.com/engineering/structural /empire-statepbuilding.htm

2. Treasures of New York City: The Flatiron Building, (WLIW Television, 2014) http://en.wikipedia.org/wiki/Flatiron_Building

3. Manhattan Company Building Designation Report, 2. http://www.nyc.gov./html/lpc/downloads/pdf/reports/4 0wallst.pdf

4. The Woolworth Building, http://en.wikipedia.org/wiki/Woolworth_Building

5. The Manhattan Company, http://skyscraper.org/TALLEST_TOWERS/t_manco.htm

6. ibid.

7. ibid

8. Jeff Glasser, New York Architecture Images – Chrysler Building,

9. http://www.nyc-architecture.com/MID/MID021.htm

10. The Skyscraper Museum: THE RISE OF WALL STREET, 40 Wall Street Construction http://skyscraper.org/EXHIBITIONS/WALL_STREET/40_w

all_3.php

11. A View on Cities, 40 Wall Street, New York City
    http://www.aviewdoncities.com/nyc/40wallstreet.htm

12. The Skyscraper Museum: THE RISE OF WALL STREET, 40
    Wall Street Construction

13. Manhattan Company Building Designation Report, 6.

14. Chrysler Building | 405 Lexington Avenue New York | History http://www.lookze.com/building.php?Address=405-Lexington-Avenue

15. ibid.

16. Chrysler Building – New World Encyclopedia
    http://www.newworldencyclopedia.org/entry/Chrysler_Building

17. ibid.

18. John J. Raskob
    http://en.wikipedia.org/wiki/John_J._Raskob

19. ibid.

20. ibid.

21. Empire State Building, Historic Construction Projects,
    http://www.generalcontractor.com/resourcs/articles/empire-state-building.asp

22. Waldorf Astoria History,

23. http://www.waldorfnewyork.com/about-the-waldorf/hotel-history.html

24. Empire state Building, Historic Construction Projects,
    http://www.generalcontractor.com/resources/articles/empire-state-building.asp

25. ibid.

26. ASCE Metroplitan Section – Empire State Building
http://www.ascemetsection.org/content/view/343/877/

27. ibid.

28. Somik Ghosh, PhD; Kenneth S. Robson, AIC, CPC, *Analyzing
the Empire State Building   Project from the Perspective
of Lean Project Delivery System* (Associated Schools of Construction)
http://ascpro0.ascweb.org/archives/cd/2014/paper/CPG
T267002014.pdf

29. Empire state Building, Historic Construction Projects

30. ibid

31. Empire State Building
http://en.wikipedia.org/wiki/Empire_State_Building

32. Somik Ghosh, PhD; Kenneth S. Robson, AIC, CPC, *Analyzing
the Empire State Building   Project from the Perspective
of Lean Project Delivery System*

33. ASCE Metroplitan section – Empire State Building

34. Empire State Building
http://en.wikipedia.org/wiki/Empire_State_Building

35. ibid.

36. Empire state Building, Historic Construction Projects

37. ASCE Metroplitan Section – Empire State Building

38. Manhattan Company Building Designation Report, 2.

39. ibid.

40. Manhattan Company Building Designation Report, 6.

41. "Pilot Lost in Fog," *New York Times*, May 21, 1946, p. 1

42. Christopher Gray, Streetscapes, (1992)
    http://www.nytimes.com/1992/11/15/realestate/
    streetscapes-40-wall-street-a-race-for-the-   skies-lost-by-
    a-spire.html

43. The Manhattan Company

44. Jeff Glasser, New York Architecture Images – Chrysler
    Building

45. David Robertson, *No Threat from Large Gorillas*. (The
    Times, April 23, 2012) "According to details prepared for
    the proposed initial public offering of Empire State   Real-
    ty Trust, the skyscraper earned $62.9 million from its ob-
    servation deck in nine months last year, compared with
    $62.6 million from the rental of office space."
    http://www.thetimes.co.uk/tto/business/industries/const
    ruction- property/article3391920.ece

46. Ed Grabianowski, *Empire State Building Completed – How
    Stuff Works*

47. Empire State Building
    http://en.wikipedia.org/wiki/Empire_State_Building "The
    famous 1951 sale of the Empire State Building to Roger L.
    Stevens...for a record $51 million was at the the highest
    price paid for a single structure in real estate history."

48. Empire State Building, Historical Timeline.
    http://www.esbnyc.com/explore/historical- timeline

49. Empire State Building
    http://en.wikipedia.org/wiki/Empire_State_Building

50. Empire State Building, Historical Timeline

51. American Society of Civil Engineers Seven Wonders
    http://www.asce.org/Content.aspx?id=2147487305

4. THE PENTAGON

1. Steve Vogel, *The Pentagon – A History* (New York: Random House, 2007) *xxii*

2. ibid.

3. Vogel, *The Pentagon,* 9

4. ibid. 16

5. ibid.

6. Vogel, *The Pentagon,* 22

7. ibid.

8. ibid. 30

9. Alfred Goldberg, (1992). *The Pentagon: The First Fifty Years.* Office of the Secretary of Defense (Government Printing Office 1992) 6-9

10. Vogel, *The Pentagon* 33

11. ibid. 39

12. Brehon B. Somervelle, Wikipedia http://en.wikipedia.org/wiki/Brehon_B_Somervelle

13. Vogel, *The Pentagon* 40

14. ibid. 89

15. Kurt Stout, "The Building of the Pentagon" | Capitol Markets http://www.capitolmarkets.com/agencies/dod/the-building-of-the-pentagon/

16. Vogel, *The Pentagon* 102

17. ibid. 124

18. ibid. 124 – 125

19. ibid. 126

20. ibid. 130

21. The Pentagon, GlobalSecurity.org
    http://www.globalsecurity.org/military/facility/pentagon.
    html

22. Vogel, *The Pentagon* 132

23. ibid. 133

24. ibid. 124

25. ibid. 147

26. ibid. 148

27. ibid. 149

28. ibid. 151

29. ibid. 161

30. ibid. 162

31. ibid. 169

32. ibid. 170

33. ibid. 176

34. ibid. 170

35. ibid. 194

36. ibid.193

37. ibid. 196

38. Steve Vogel, *The Pentagon – A History* (New York: Random House, 2007) 209

39. ibid.

40. ibid. 216

41. The Pentagon, Wikipedia
http://en.wikipedia.org/wiki/The_Pentagon

42. The Pentagon | Infoplease
http://www.infoplease.com/spot/pentagon1.html

43. The Pentagon, Wikipedia

44. The Pentagon | Infoplease

45. Steve Vogel, *The Pentagon – A History* 253

46. ibid

47. Steve Vogel, *The Pentagon – A History* 190

48. ibid. 189

49. Steve Vogel, *The Pentagon – A History* 253

50. John Kennedy Ohl (1994). *Supplying the Troops: General Somervell and American Logistics in World War II.* (DeKalb Illinois: Northern Illinois Press, 1994).

5. THE SS UNITED STATES

1. Carl c. Cutler, *Greyhounds of the Sea* (United States Naval Institute/Patrick Northants, 1984) 65-68

2. Cunard Line, Wikipedia
http://en.wikipedia.org/wiki/Cunard_Line p.8

3. Blue Riband, Wikipedia
http://en.wikipedia.org/wiki/Blue_Riband

4. Arnold Kludas, *Record breakers of the North Atlantic, Blue Riband Liners 1838–1952.*   (London: Chatham, 2000).

5. ibid.

6. Blue Riband, Wikipedia

7. Steven Ujifusa, *A Man And His Ship* (New York: Simon & Schuster, 2012) 61

8. Merchant Marine, Wikipedia
http://en.wikipedia.org/wiki/Merchant_Marine

9. Merchant Marine Act of 1936, Wikipedia
http://en.wikipedia.org/wiki/Merchant_Marine_Act_of_1936

10. Steven Ujifusa, *A Man And His Ship* 22

11. ibid. 3

12. ibid. 28 & 30

13. ibid. 33

14. Arnold Kludas, *Record breakers of the North Atlantic, Blue Riband Liners 1838–1952.*

15. ibid.

16. William Francis Gibbs, Wikipedia
http://en.wikipedia.org/wiki/William_Francis_Gibbs

17. Steven Ujifusa, *A Man And His Ship* 60

18. Frank O. Braynard & Robert Hudson Westover, *SS United States: Fastest Ship in the   World* (Paducah, KY: Turner, 2002) 17

19. William Horgard, "Biographical Memoir of David Watson Taylor, 1864 – 1940," *National Academy of Sciences of the United States of America Biographical Memoirs,* vol   22, 7th Memoir, presented to the academy at the annual meeting, 1941 p. 135

20. Model and Notes, "1,000 ft. Superliner, 'Project S-171,' Proposed American Passenger   Ship," accession 1971.0074.000001, collection of the Mariner's Museum, Newport News,   VA

21. Alva Johnson, "The Mysterious Mr. Gibbs – II," *Saturday Evening Post,* January 27,1945,   p. 97

22. Frank O. Braynard, *Leviathan,* vol 1 (New York: South Street Seaport Museum, 1972)   113

23. Herbert Hartley, *Home is the Sailor* (Birmingham, AL: Vulcan Press, 1955) 78 – 70, as   quoted in Braynard, *The World's Greatest Ship,* vol 1 p. 125

24. *New York American,* Feb 14, 1920, as quotd in Braynard, *The World's Greatest Ship,* vol   2, p. 24

25. Braynard, *The World's Greatest Ship,* vol 2, p. 90

26. Steven Ujifusa, *A Man And His Ship* 91

27. SS Malolo, Wikipedia
http://en.wikipedia.org/wiki/SS_Malolo

28. Steven Ujifusa, *A Man And His Ship* 141

29. ibid. 125

30. ibid. 144

31. William Francis Gibbs, Wikipedia
http://en.wikipedia.org/wiki/William_Francis_Gibbs

32. SS America, Wikipedia,
http://en.wikipedia.org/wiki/SS_America_%281939%29

33. Steven Ujifusa, *A Man And His Ship* 193

34. ibid. 197

35. ibid. 200

36. ibid. 202

37. ibid.

38. SS United States, Wikipedia,
http://en.wikipedia.org/wiki/SS_United_States

39. Steven Ujifusa, *A Man And His Ship* 203

40. "Mr. Gibbs Baby," *New Yorker,* November 16, 1957

41. Steven Ujifusa, *A Man And His Ship* 353

42. ibid. 215

43. ibid. 217

44. ibid. 215

45. ibid. 220

46. ibid. 221

47. Frank O. Braynard & Robert Hudson Westover, *SS United States: Fastest Ship in the   World* p. 36

48. Raymond Foster Options, Ltd, *The SS United States from Dream to Reality* (Newport   News VA: Mariner's Musuem, 1992)

49. Steven Ujifusa, *A Man And His Ship* 229

50. ibid

51. ibid. 234

52. Frank O. Braynard & Robert Hudson Westover, *SS United States: Fastest Ship in the   World* p. 43

53. George Horne, *"Biggest U.S. Liner 'Launched' in Dock; New Superliner After Being Christened Yesterday"*. (The New York Times. 24 June 1951) http://query.nytimes.com/gst/abstract.html?res=9 A07E4DB1631E33ABC4C51DFB06683

54. Steven Ujifusa, *A Man And His Ship* 244

55. ibid. 264

56. ibid. 355

57. ibid. 310

58. ibid. 314

59. SS United States, A Spacious, Modern Ship http://www.ss-united- states.com/spec06d.html

60. Steven Ujifusa, *A Man And His Ship* 319

61. William Francis Gibbs, Wikipedia http://en.wikipedia.org/wiki/William_Francis_Gibbs

62. Steven Ujifusa, *A Man And His Ship* 369

63. SS United States Conservancy – Our Board
http://www.ssusc.org/the-conservancy/our- board/

6. A LOSS OF DOMINANCE

1. Grand Coulee Dam,
http://en.wikipedia.org/wiki/Grand_Coulee_Dam

2. Shasta Dam, http://en.wikipedia.org/wiki/shasta_Dam

3. Leonard Ortolano & Kao Cushing, *Grand Coulee Dam and the Columbia Basin Project –   USA* (Capetown, South Africa: World Commission on Dams, 2000) 59

4. Shasta Dam

5. ESD Designing Building Systems for Kingdom Tower,
http://www.businesswire.com/news/home/20110805005 139/en/ESD-Designing-Building-   Systems-Kingdom-Tower#.VUJnOflViko

6. Adrian Smith – Architect ,
http://en.wikipedia.org/wiki/Adrian_Smith_%28architect %29

7. John Augustus Roebling,
http://en.wikipedia.org/wiki/John_A._Roebling

8. The World's New Largest Building is Four Times the Size of Vatican City,

9. http://qz.com/100639/china-chengdu-world-new-largest-building-is-four-times-the-size-   of-vatican-city/

ANALYZING THE DECLINE

1. Reclamation, Managing Water in the West,
http://www.usbr.gov/main/about/

2. Glen Canyon Dam,
   http://en.wikipedia.org/wiki/Glen_Canyon_Dam#Continui
   ng_debates

3. United States Bureau of Reclamation - History
   http://en.wikipedia.org/wiki/United_States_Bureau_of_Rec
   lamation

4. Big Think, *How the West is Owned,*
   http://bigthink.com/strange-maps/291-federal-lands-in-
   the-us

5. *On the Duty of Civil Disobedience,*
   http://www.constitution.org/civ/civildis.htm

6. James C. Humes, *The Wit & Wisom of Ronald Reagan* (Washington D.C.: Regnery 2007)   19

7. Joseph J. Ellis, *American Sphinx* (New York: Alfred A. Knopf,
   1996)

8. United States Federal Executive Departments,
   http://en.wikipedia.org/wiki/United_States_federal_execut
   ive_departments

9. The Growth of Government, 1980 – 2012,
   http://www.forbes.com/sites/mikepatton/2013/01/24/th
   e-growth-of-the-federal-   government-1980-to-2012/

10. Competitive Enterprise Institute, *New Data: Code of Federal
    Regulations Expanding,   Faster Pace under Obama*
    https://cei.org/blog/new-data-code-federal-regulations-
    expanding-faster-pace-under-obama

11. Philip K Howard, *The Death of Common Sense* (New York:
    Random House, 1994) 172

12. Sir John Glubb, *The Fate of Empires and Search for Survival*
    (Edinburgh, Scotland: William Blackwood & Sons, Ltd.,
    1976-77) 20

13. ibid.

14. US National Debt Clock – Real Time
http://www.usdebtclock.org/

15. ibid.

16. US Federal Deficit Definition,
http://www.usgovernmentspending.com/federal_deficit_c
hart.html

17. Cal Thomas, *Decadence leads to decline, and America shows the telltale signs*
http://www.washingtontimes.com/news/2014/de
c/29/cal-thomas-america-shows-decline-   signs-of-
empires-/

8. CAN AMERICA BOUNCE BACK

1. Jeff Thomas, International Man *The Constitution, Past & Present*   http://www.internationalman.com/

2. James Rickards, *Currency Wars, The Making of the Next Global Crisis* (New York: Penguin Books, 2011) 200

3. ibid.

4. Jim Rickards Strategic Intelligence, *30 "Snowflakes"That Could Trigger the Next Financial Avalanche"*
http://agorafinancial.com

5. John Locke, http://en.wikipedia.org/wiki/John_Locke

6. State of Emergency,
http://en.wikipedia.org/wiki/State_of_emergency

7. Executive Order 6102,
http://en.wikipedia.org/wiki/Executive_Order_6102

8. Judicial Procedures Reform Act 1937,

http://en.wikipedia.org/wiki/Judicial_Procedures_Reform_
Bill_of_1937

9. Coup D'etat,
    http://en.wikipedia.org/wiki/Coup_d%27%C3%A9tat

10. Sir John Glubb, *The Fate of Empires and Search for Survival,*
    20

11. Steve Vogel, *The Pentagon* 300

12. ibid. 358

13. Oh Captain! My Captain! The Poetry Foundation,
    http://www.poetryfoundation.org/poem/17474

Made in the USA
Las Vegas, NV
19 December 2022

63651665R00098